Praise for *Working Relationships*

"*Working Relationships* is the best book I have seen on improving relationships within organizations, leading to higher productivity and comfort with others. Bob Wall is an expert in team building and in helping people develop their potential."

    Steve Simmons, President, Simmons Management Systems,
    and Author, *Measuring Emotional Intelligence*

"This book takes a straightforward approach to understanding the dynamics of interpersonal relationships in the workplace and offers useful step-by-step tools on how to successfully prepare for and face your most dreaded discussions."

    Beth A. Taylor, Human Resources Manager, Zetec, Inc.

"Readers will benefit from Bob Wall's experience, research, and unfailing ability to put workplace drama into perspective. I've used his exercises with all levels of the organization and have been hailed as a 'hero' for putting his ideas to work."

    Alayne Fardella, Manager, Training and Organizational
    Development, *The Seattle Times*

"If you've ever worked on a team gone awry, had to put up with a jerky co-worker, or fumbled for a way to raise a problem with your boss, *Working Relationships* is the book for you."

    Terry Byington, Executive Director, Washington Council,
    American Electronics Association

"With insight and candor, Bob Wall demonstrates the importance of building productive relationships in today's organizations. This book is loaded with tools to help make that happen."

    Helm Lehmann, Author, *Driver's Ed for Today's Managers*

"*Working Relationships* is a practical guide featuring worthwhile exercises and real-world examples. The techniques you will find in this book helped my management team turn its leadership relationships around."

Ed Kommers, President,
University Mechanical Contractors, Inc.

"A practical guide to help us see that work is not our life and learn how to make a segment of life more fulfilling."

Lori Christenson, Vice President, Everett Mutual Bank,
and President, I-Pro Inc.

"An insightful book that clearly defines personal and professional relationships in the workplace and how they impact organizational effectiveness and team development. It offers a good practical approach with exercises to resolving and managing relationships between individuals."

Fred J. Dal Broi, Deputy Production Director,
The Arizona Republic

"An engaging read laced with tools and concepts that really make a difference. If you have a job that requires working successfully with other people, you MUST read this book!"

Maxine Hayes, M.D., Assistant Secretary,
Community and Family Health, and Acting Health Officer,
Washington State Department of Health

Working Relationships

The Simple Truth
About Getting Along
with Friends
and Foes at Work

Bob Wall

Davies-Black Publishing
Palo Alto, California

Published by Davies-Black Publishing, an imprint of Consulting Psychologists Press, Inc., 3803 East Bayshore Road, Palo Alto, CA 94303; 800-624-1765.

Special discounts on bulk quantities of Davies-Black books are available to corporations, professional associations, and other organizations. For details, contact the Director of Book Sales at Davies-Black Publishing, an imprint of Consulting Psychologists Press, Inc., 3803 East Bayshore Road, Palo Alto, CA 94303; 650-691-9123; fax 650-623-9271.

Visit the Davies-Black Publishing web site at www.daviesblack.com.

04 03 02 01 00   11 10 9 8 7 6 5 4 3
Printed in the United States of America

Library of Congress Cataloging-in-Publication Data
    Wall, Bob (Bob Lee)
  Working relationships : the simple truth about getting along with friends and foes at work / Bob Wall.
      p. cm.
  Includes index.
  ISBN 0-89106-133-9 (paperback)
  1. Office politics. 2. Psychology, Industrial. 3. Interpersonal relations. 4. Interpersonal communication. I. Title.
HF5386.5.W35   1999
650.1'3—dc21

                                                             99-22730

FIRST EDITION
First printing 1999

Dedicated to the memory of Robert S. Solum

Contents

Part One The Tangled Web of Relationships in the Workplace

Part Two Fixing the Relationships That Are Not Working

Part Three Making the Good Relationships Even Better

Exercises

Preface

Welcome to a conversation about work. This is a book written for anyone who works for a living and finds the interpersonal side of work puzzling or challenging at times. You may be thinking, "Well, who doesn't?" Almost everyone experiences difficult relationships at work. One troublesome relationship can ruin what might otherwise be very enjoyable and fulfilling work. If you can't seem to get along with a co-worker, it can ruin your day. If you can't get along with your boss, you may find yourself looking for another job. Being able to build effective working relationships is one of the most important factors in determining both your success and your satisfaction at work. So what are you to do when you just can't seem to make an important relationship work? This book will provide you with answers to that question.

Behind Closed Doors

I am about to tell you more about myself than you probably want to know. But what I do for a living is the source of almost everything you are about to read in this book. So bear with me for a moment while I tell you a little bit about my work. I want you to know that I am not an ivory tower theorist who writes about work without engaging with people who actually *do* work. I have been lucky enough to create a way to make a living talking to other people about what *they* do for a living.

I have been a full-time consultant since 1980, specializing in the assessment and development of people and teams within organizations. My training and development projects usually begin with an "organizational snapshot," a series of private conversations with managers and staff from my client's company. My intent is to learn as much as an outsider can about what life looks like to those inside the organization. I want to hear about what people love about their jobs as well as what concerns them and what changes they might like to see made. I also ask for their assessment of the people they work with, especially people in management positions.

Given the promise of confidentiality and the invitation to talk about whatever might be on their minds, people are usually eager to unload.

And what do they want to talk about? Other people. They tell me about problems with managers and supervisors. I hear about conflicts with co-workers and problems working with other departments. I hear about long-standing personality conflicts and the difficulty of resolving emotionally charged issues. I then spend time with individuals and teams, working on solutions to any problems that surfaced in the interviews. I also lead workshops and have worked with participants in leadership and team development seminars all across the country. All told, I have spent literally thousands of hours with individuals and with groups, exploring the issues of concern to them and developing tools to enable people to work.

I wanted to tell you a little about my work because I want you to understand that the information and communication strategies you'll find in this book are based on what I have learned from people I've met in consulting and training projects. On my own merits alone, I have little to offer in the form of wisdom that can help you find ways to be happier and more successful in your working life. But I do have something of great value to offer you in the pages that follow. I've spent years learning about work from people in all walks of life, from company presidents to blue-collar workers. The stories in this book are their stories. The lessons offered in these pages belong to them. I see myself as a conduit, privileged to be in the position to be able to share what I have learned working with so many people just like yourself.

The information and communication strategies presented in this book have undergone development for almost two decades. These materials have been taken out into the workplace by my clients and continually refined, based on what has and hasn't worked as they applied these strategies in coping with the challenges of their work. There is not a single concept or skill in this book that hasn't stood the test of application in the world of work. The principles and tools you will find in this book will work for you.

An Overview

The first section of the book examines relationships in the workplace. One of the most important distinctions to make when we work with people is sorting out the mix of personal and professional relationships. We will be looking at how to bring clarity to these relationships in a way that allows us to work with people, disagree without taking things so personally, and still maintain the friendships that add so much to the quality of our working lives.

The next section presents a practical methodology for understanding and building teamwork. Every company talks about the importance of teamwork. In job interviews, most of us profess to be team players. Unfortunately, most people arrive in the workplace without a practical understanding of teamwork, how to build an effective team, and how to diagnose the problem when teamwork breaks down. This section offers a simple model for understanding teamwork and points to the agreements that need to be in place for people to be able to work together effectively. The model also becomes a lifesaver in times of conflict, providing a way of more accurately putting your finger on what is going on and what you need to do to fix it.

The first two sections can be thought of as offering "thinking skills" that will enable you to understand the complex challenges of working relationships and maintaining effective teamwork with your co-workers. The third section gets to the heart of teamwork…communication. It is one thing to understand teamwork and conflict. It is quite another to be able to talk about it, especially when teamwork has gone south and relationships are close to the breaking point. This section offers you tried-and-true methods for preparing to raise issues and engaging in conversations that make things happen—all the while with an eye on maintaining your personal and professional relationships with the people involved.

The last section of the book addresses what you can do to clarify your aspirations and seek out the kind of personal feedback that will help you see yourself more clearly and make any necessary course corrections. We will end our study of working relationships with strategies for maintaining more satisfying personal connections with people you think of as both friends and colleagues.

A Conversation About Work

I have done my best to make this book an enjoyable and easy reading experience. I have done everything I can to avoid producing a dry, academic presentation of what can be a complex topic. The emphasis in these pages is on your application of what you are learning. The book offers practical strategies and suggests things for you to do that will prove well worth the time you invest in them.

In the months it took me to complete the manuscript, I thought about it as a conversation in which you and I were discussing working relationships and some of the lessons we have learned to make them richer, more meaningful, and more productive. But conversations require both people to be engaged in the discussion. Otherwise what might look like a conversation is really just a long monologue, with one person doing all the talking. Reading this book in that way might be interesting but ultimately might not make all that much difference in your life. Therefore I have designed the book to be more like a workshop in written form. Good workshops, especially those designed to improve skills, have to involve participants in three ways:

- First, the trainer must provide information to help broaden the participants' understanding of the topic being explored.
- Second, the workshop should include opportunities for participants to explore their own attitudes and beliefs about the topic of the event. If they are to use what is being taught, the event should lead participants through an exploration of the value of the content being delivered and of how existing attitudes and beliefs can either promote or inhibit the transfer of training to situations outside the workshop.
- Finally, the workshop must include skills and opportunities to practice and sharpen those skills.

Your Part

In a book, the best I can do is provide information and strategies that can make a difference in your working relationships. The rest is up to you. I have included exercises for you to explore your feelings and beliefs about working relationships. There are many skill application exercises, designed to prepare you to take action and make things happen for yourself and for your company. If you follow the directions and devote time to doing the written exercises and conversational assignments, this book offers you the opportunity to create a turning point in your life at work.

Many of the exercises direct you to write about very personal topics. Others ask you to identify relationships at work in need of repair. You may choose to do the exercises in a journal or at your computer. By all means do the work I ask you to do. Most of the exercises are short and easy to complete. The time you invest in completing the exercises will be more than worth it.

Over the years I have been blessed to get to know people in all walks of life working at every level of their organizations, from company presidents to the people who actually do the work. Starting with an interest in developing practical communication strategies stripped clean of any unnecessary psychological jargon, my work has enabled me to spend untold hours talking with people about their work, learning from them what works and what doesn't work in the real world of the workplace.

What you will find in this book has stood the test of time. The concepts and communication strategies have been developed and refined based on what I have learned from my clients in countless training rooms and consulting projects over the course of my career. I want to make you a promise: this book will work for you if you do your part. The tools you will find in these pages will help you build more effective working relationships.

Acknowledgments

This book could not have been written without the support and patience of my wife, Adrienne. Through all the months of work, her encouragement kept me going. This was especially true when I was working on the proposal for the book, a project that was much shorter than the book itself but took me three times longer to complete. Sometimes loving support takes the form of a well-placed kick in the seat of the pants. Then came a beautiful summer in Seattle when, facing a deadline, I spent so many weekends and evenings writing rather than doing all the things that make this area such a pleasant place to live. For her understanding and willingness to let me do the work that had to be done, I am grateful beyond my ability to put my feelings into words.

This book is dedicated to the memory of Bob Solum, my late friend and colleague. Bob and I spent years at a blackboard in our office, developing much of the material in this book and then taking it out into the workplace to be tested by our clients. There is so much of Bob, and of Mark Sobol, the coauthor of my first book, *The Mission-Driven Organization,* in these pages that I know this book could not have been written on my merits alone. I am grateful for their friendship and the intellectual stimulation that proved to be so influential in the unfolding of my career.

If you are lucky, you will meet one person in your lifetime whose influence and contribution change the course of your life. I got lucky. I met Art Turock in the 1970s when I volunteered as a trainer in his Interpersonal Skills Training Project for the state of Iowa. Art's patience, coaching, and intellectual rigor made me the trainer I am today. I had no way of knowing at the time that my work with Art would lead to a career in the pursuit of simple approaches to complex interpersonal challenges. Without Art's influence, this book, and my work in the field, would not have been possible.

In writing my proposal, two other people gave me support and input that influenced the direction of the work—Beth Taylor and Marion Terrell. I am grateful for the time they invested in reading the draft of the proposal and for their insightful suggestions that shaped the project.

To the members of my breakfast club at the Charlestown Café: Thanks for all the encouragement and support throughout the preparation of this manuscript. Couldn't have done it without you!

One person provided me with the inspiration to finish the proposal—Helm Lehmann. I followed him as he was finishing his own book, *Driver's Ed for Today's Managers*. His dedication in completing his book confronted me with my own commitment. Was I going to get the proposal finished or not? Conversations with him motivated me to break through my reluctance to invest the time I knew it was going to take. For that I am grateful.

This project would never have been completed without the enthusiasm and support of my agent, John Willig. From my very first contact with him, I knew I had found someone who understood what I was up to and who would not be satisfied until my project was ready for prime time. For his representation and encouragement, I am grateful.

Finally, I have to thank the hundreds of people who have let me into their lives in training rooms and consulting projects over the years. It is their willingness to explore work and working relationships that made this book possible.

About the Author

I have been fascinated for many years by the complexity of relationships and what it takes to make them work. Interested in both individual and group process, I focused on the study of psychology in my college days, completing a master's degree in that field. I then moved on to do work on a Ph.D. degree in clinical psychology. Along the way, I became a trainer for an interpersonal skills training project in Iowa.

My involvement in creating communication strategies and designing training events proved to be a turning point in my career. I was just about finished with my Ph.D. program when I was presented with a choice: complete the work on my dissertation or join some friends from the training project in moving to Seattle to start a consulting business. It was a no-brainer. I left Iowa City for Seattle in 1980 and have never looked back.

Since that time, I have devoted my career to the study of working relationships, looking at what it takes for people to work effectively together.

Chapter One

Working Together

It is hard to imagine a job that does not require interaction with people. Most of us, for instance, have a boss to deal with, requiring ongoing communication and an understanding of what we are to do and how we are supposed to do it. I was doing a consulting project with a high-tech manufacturing company and was talking to a team member about the company and how he felt about his job. "I really like what I do for a living," he said. "This job enables me to put my training to use and I'm learning new skills as I work on the new product we are developing. In some ways, this job is everything that I could have hoped for."

"Then why are you updating your resume and starting to look for a new job?" I asked. Here was his response:

If the work were all I had to focus on, I'd be in great shape. But the personal climate here is awful. My boss is such a jerk. She almost never communicates, at least about anything positive. All she does is focus on minor mistakes. I feel like she is constantly looking over my shoulder, waiting to jump on me about something I do wrong. And her definition of "wrong" is doing anything any other way than she would have done it. I don't have room to breathe. I think it might be time for me to move on.

Most of us also have co-workers, requiring coordination of efforts, sharing resources, and managing the complications of working together. Another conversation I had with an employee on a different project focused on the problems a person was having with her co-workers:

There is so much tension on my unit. Most of it is caused by one of the nurses who is so hard to get along with. Nothing we do pleases her. She is always complaining about her hours and her workload. When something goes wrong, it is never her fault. She is always looking for someone else to blame. Because I'm new here, I'm the one who gets stuck working with her when she needs help. I'm tired of listening to her complain about the administration and problems in her personal life. With an attitude like hers, I'll bet she has problems at home. Nothing I learned in nursing school prepared me to deal with people like her. I am just about to the end of my rope and I don't know what to do about it.

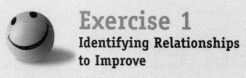
This is a book about relationships in the workplace and how to make them work for you. We will be doing a great deal of work on how to understand working relationships and what you can do to improve relationships in need of repair. Exercise 1 asks you to reflect on people at work and to identify relationships in need of improvement.

We do things because it pays off in some way. Not dealing with relationship issues pays off in some way. For example, we get to avoid taking the risk of starting a conversation that might not go well. We may also be avoiding taking responsibility for the relationship and finding a degree of satisfaction in blaming the other person. What is the payoff you get for not talking about your concerns? Is it worth the price you pay in terms of the impact on your effectiveness and your satisfaction?

Don't do anything yet. We will be looking at how to prepare for just these kinds of conversations. For now, ask yourself if you are open to the possibility of taking action to improve these relationships.

Working Effectively with Others

Being able to work effectively with people is one of the most important factors in determining our success on the job. Certainly, mastering the technical side of your job is important. If you are an airline pilot, you'd better be able to put the plane on the runway—every time—regardless of how well you get along with the rest of the flight crew. You would never recommend a doctor to a friend by saying, "Dr. Jones is not much of a doctor, but he's a nice guy. I think you'll like him."

But as important as technical mastery may be, it may not be enough to guarantee success. I have seen technically skilled people lose their positions because they were unable to get along with the rest of the team. In a survey by Marlene Lozada ("Social Misfits, Workplace Outcasts," *Vocational Educational Journal,* vol. 71, 1996) that looked into reasons why people get fired, deficient job skills played only a minor role. Ninety percent of firings were the result of poor attitudes, inappropriate behavior, and difficulties with interpersonal relationships. Think about that for a moment. Nine times out of ten, people who lost their job had the technical ability it took to do the job. They could not get along with other people or they had "attitudinal problems," which, in my experience, usually show up in the form of disrupted relationships anyway. Others may not go so far as to lose their jobs, but their inability to work with people may put a lid on their promotion. Some highly skilled people stay where they are in the organization because it is all too apparent that they would make terrible managers.

Being good isn't enough if you can't work with people.

Other studies have supported the importance of developing good interpersonal skills. Companies look for people who demonstrate the ability to do their jobs well. Then they promote them with the hope that they can manage other people who are doing similar work. Once promoted, what often separates the successful from the not-so-successful managers is their mastery of interpersonal skills. Success in leadership positions requires the ability to work with and through other people. If you are already in management, you know how important it is to be able to work with a wide variety of people. You may not yet be in a leadership position but see that as the next step in developing your career. If so, you will certainly want to continue demonstrating that you can do your job well. But you will also need to show that you can work well with other people.

Technical abilities may get you into management, but it takes interpersonal abilities to stay there.

Job Satisfaction

Our capacity to get along with other people is important for yet another reason—job satisfaction. We devote a huge proportion of our adult life to work. The quality of our life at work is a critical factor in determining the quality of our entire life. If you work forty hours a week, you are likely to devote at least eighty to ninety thousand hours of your adult life to work! Your work had better be gratifying if you expect to have a full and satisfying life.

One of the most important factors in determining how people like their jobs is the quality of the relationships they find there. No matter how much we might like a particular task the job requires of us, it is hard to stay excited about a job if we get along terribly with our boss or our co-workers.

Good working relationships **make** even the **worst job bearable.**

On the other hand, working with great people will make even a routine job more enjoyable. We spend a great deal of time with people on the job. On workdays, most of us spend more of our waking hours with our co-workers than we do with our families. We may also work with some of the same people for years, day in and day out. So the quality of these relationships is vitally important to us. Spend a few moments reflecting on the questions posed in exercise 2.

It's Never Been Easy

You would think that we would have figured out how to work together by now. After all, we have been doing it for a very long time. But I am willing to bet that we started having trouble with this when we first started gathering together in groups. I can picture the cave dwellers sitting around a fire in a cold, damp cave, complaining about the guy who didn't do his share on the hunt that day. And from the dawn of time,

Exercise 2
How Co-Workers Contribute to Your Working Life

- Think about two or three co-workers whose presence makes your work more enjoyable. List three to five of their personal qualities that leave you feeling that way about them.

- If you could consistently be the kind of person you would like to be, what are the qualities you would like for your co-workers to appreciate about you?

- Identify one thing you could do today to make a co-worker's day a bit brighter.

- Now do it!

there have always been people trying to tell other people what to do: "Who does he think he is, trying to tell me how to throw a spear? I've forgotten more about hunting than he will ever know!"

Working together still isn't easy. The truth is, almost everyone has times when dealing with people is one of the most aggravating things about working. We may have a co-worker who is difficult to get along with. We may have a boss who is hard to get to know and almost impossible to please. Or we may have occasional problems working with customers. Working with people can be frustrating. It can get so bad that interpersonal problems may be the one thing that keeps us from finding satisfaction in the job we have at the time. We may like the work itself and the customers we serve, and we may even enjoy working with most of our co-workers. But one difficult relationship at work can ruin your whole day—day after day.

Making Things Happen

I have talked to many people in all walks of life about things that are frustrating them at work. When people talk about their frustrations, they usually focus on other people as the source of their problems. Managers complain about people who are not performing as expected. Employees complain about managers who are not sharing information or delegating authority. And everyone complains about co-workers, talking about individuals who don't pull their own weight or people who are hard to get along with. At some point in the conversation, I always ask, "Have you talked to this person about this? Have you tried to solve this problem?" More often than not, the answer is "Are you kidding? I can't talk to him (or her) about that!"

Making things work at work begins with your willingness to step forward and make things happen. When things at work are not going as well as you would like them to, I think the only useful question to ask is, "How am I the source of this? What am I doing—or not doing—that is contributing to things turning out the way they are?"

When things are not going the way you want, it is all too easy to look for someone to blame—your boss, a co-worker, "management," or the ever-popular "politics."

The one common denominator **in every mess** you find yourself in **is you.**

But the conversation we are having about your life at work is not about the other person. It is about you. There is almost always something you are doing—or not doing—that is playing a part in things turning out the way they are. Sometimes I hate taking my own advice. When something doesn't go my way, I would prefer to blame some other person as the source of the problem. I must confess that I may even find a certain satisfaction in complaining to friends about what a raw deal I'm getting. But if I look carefully, I almost always find something I could have done differently. Or I will find something I should have done but did not do that is contributing to the situation.

Are you willing to own your piece of the **problem,** or do you prefer to **"be right"** and blame other people?

Not long ago I had a reminder of this in my personal life. My wife and I bought a house and had it remodeled. We hired a painting contractor who did such a poor job that we had to terminate our contract with him, hire another painter, and pay the expense of having the interior painting redone. Let me assure you, this incident was good for a lot of justifiable complaining to friends. One day I was talking to a client about the question, "How am I the source of this?" I started thinking about my self-righteous anger at the painter and looking at my role in how things had turned out. My fingerprints were all over the situation. We should have interviewed more painters and gotten more bids. We should have checked references. We should have inspected his work more closely from the very beginning of the project. In all kinds of ways, I played a role in things turning out the way they did. As a friend of mine once said so well, it is impossible to get dumped on unless you first properly position yourself.

Our circumstances are always about *us,* not the other guy. Suppose you do not get enough coaching and feedback from your boss. Have you asked for it? Maybe you have a staff member whose performance is less than satisfactory. Have you been offering this person corrective coaching? Maybe you have a co-worker who is hard to work with. Have you tried to reach out and resolve any issues affecting your relationship?

Perhaps an even more important question to ask in any of these situations at work is, "Am I willing to look at my role in this situation, or do I just want to keep on blaming other people?" Looking at our own role is not just a way to blame ourselves and feel bad about how we do things. On the contrary, once we start to look at how we participated in

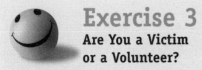

Exercise 3
Are You a Victim or a Volunteer?

Identify two examples of recent events at work that left you feeling angry, frustrated, or otherwise upset. Describe each incident, exploring the following questions in sequence:

• Who else is involved in this situation and what are your feelings about them?

• In what ways do you feel other people are at fault in this situation?

• In what ways did you participate in determining the outcome of this situation? Are there things you did or things you didn't do that played a role in the outcome?

• What could you do in the future to avoid the same outcome in similar situations?

the way things turned out, we will begin to identify things we can do to resolve this situation and avoid similar problems in the future. Try the exercise above.

Talking to Each Other

Let me tell you something about consultants, at least consultants who do the kind of work I like to do. My work isn't all that complicated. All I ever do is talk to people behind closed doors and find out what people are *not* talking about. Then I bring people together in pairs or teams and say something brilliant like, "Um, it looks to me like you need to talk." Of course, I do bring a body of information and communication skills to help make the conversation productive, but in reality you don't really need consultants like me. Everything you need to make your job start getting better is just a conversation away from movement in the right direction. Everything your company needs to be great is already present in the hearts and minds of the people who work there. But all too often, these ideas go unexpressed and unheard, in part because we sometimes do not know how to talk to each other about work.

If people like you would just start talking to each other, people like me would have to go find a real

> **Silence** is deadlier than open **conflict.** Conflict, even **poorly** expressed, can at least **be dealt with.**

Exercise 4
Do You Have a Conversation That Is Not Happening?

- List three situations in your company that would get better if only the right people would get together to talk and listen to each other.

- Why do you suppose these conversations are not happening?

- List at least one situation where you could possibly be the one to step forward to start a conversation that is dying to happen.

- What is holding you back?

job. It's *silence* that kills organizations. Conflict, even poorly handled, may even be preferable. At least we'd be talking to each other, and some good might come out of that. Do you have some conversations that are waiting to happen? Reflect on the questions posed in exercise 4.

Working with other people may be challenging, but it does not have to be impossible. I've spent nearly twenty years studying the interpersonal aspects of work, and I want you to know that there is a better way.

Part One

The Tangled Web of Relationships in the Workplace

Chapter Two

Friends and Colleagues

Our relationships at work are complicated by the fact that we have two relationships with many of our co-workers. One is personal, the other professional. The purpose of personal relationships, on or off the job, is to establish some form of personal intimacy. These relationships have a lot to do with our personal feelings about each other. We may enjoy spending time with someone because we share common interests, we feel comfortable with each other, and we enjoy talking to each other. Personal relationships at work can be very important to us. Some of us work for years with the same group of people. Given the amount of time we spend with co-workers, comfortable and supportive personal relationships can make work all the more enjoyable.

> **Personal** relationships at **work** are important for **friendship** and mutual **support.**

Some of our personal relationships at work will be quite casual. With some people, we may talk about our weekends or interests we may have in common. We share jokes or pass on the latest rumors we have heard about something that is going on in the company. We may never see each other outside the job, yet the personal comfort and rapport we find with each other make the work more enjoyable.

Other relationships at work go far beyond casual conversations in the break room. We sometimes connect with people at work in a very significant way. We may develop friendships that last far longer than our stay at any particular job. Many people date or even marry someone they first met on the job.

Think for a moment about other jobs you held prior to your current position. You probably remember certain people with real affection. It may be someone who had a particularly outrageous sense of humor. Or it may be someone who seemed to always be in an optimistic mood, whose approach to work and to life made him or her a joy to spend time with. The opportunity to work with people we care about adds richness and joy to the quality of our working life.

Unfortunately, some of our relationships are not so pleasant. Not liking someone is also a form of personal relationship. We are thrown into relationships with all kinds of people when we work for a living. We inevitably will have co-workers we would never choose as friends, or even as acquaintances. Nevertheless, there they are, day after day, at the desk next to ours or on the job site. If we had our choice, we would cut some of these people out of our lives, never to have them darken our doorway again. But work is work, and there you have it. When we take a job, our co-workers are part of the package.

Companies do not bring people together to form support groups—the primary **purpose** of working relationships is to **accomplish work.**

When we work with people, like them or not, we have a second relationship to build with them. This relationship overlaps with the personal relationship we may have with the same people. Professional relationships exist for one purpose and one purpose only—to get the job done. That is why we are in a relationship in the first place. Companies do not bring people together to be friends. We are not there to develop some form of an extended family. Our primary purpose is to accomplish work, and the company is depending on us to be able to work together to make that happen.

Personal and professional relationships involve two fundamentally different ways of relating to the same person. Having two kinds of relationships with the same people sets us up for trouble in the following ways:

- Failure to make the distinction about what is personal and what is professional is one of the most common sources of breakdown in relationships in the workplace.
- Personal and professional relationships have different purposes.
- Personal and professional relationships require different methods of communication.

Sorting Out the Complexity of Relationships at Work

In theory, sorting out personal and professional relationships at work sounds simple. Work is work. Personal is personal. So what's the problem? If we could easily keep these two relationships separate in our own minds, it would be a giant step toward our being able to work together effectively. Unfortunately, the blend of personal and professional sometimes gets hopelessly confused and creates problems for people at work. Even people with the very best of intentions find themselves stumbling over this critical distinction about working relationships.

"We're Just One Big Happy Family"

When I am getting to know business leaders at the start of a consulting project, I always ask them about what they do to create an environment in which people feel good about the work they are doing and the company they work for. Some of them get almost misty-eyed when they talk about their company and the people in it. They talk about how much the people in the company care for each other. They talk about holiday celebrations and the picnics they have in the summertime. They talk in glowing terms about the warm family feeling that marks the culture of their organization. Sometimes they sound as if they are talking about their own children. Much like loving parents, they sometimes go to extraordinary lengths to support people personally, going out of their way to assist them in times of crisis.

I admire the motivation of leaders who speak in such loving, human terms about their organization and the people who make it work. While they clearly are committed to running a business and make a profit in doing so, they have managed to stay in touch with some of the deeper, more human values of life. Unfortunately, these same owners and leaders are unintentionally setting themselves up to be a disappointment to the very people they have such strong feelings about. Their emphasis on building close, personal connections with people can lead to unrealistic expectations. Sooner or later, difficult decisions must be made for the good of the business. Economic pressures may lead to a

Emphasizing "warm family feelings" almost **inevitably results** in unreasonable and **unmet expectations.**

reduction in hours or in the number of staff employed in the business. Staffing requirements may require assigning people to shifts or hours they don't like. Promotions will be made, leaving those not chosen feeling that their personal desires were not taken into consideration. Or, problems in performance may result in corrective action that gets taken as a personal affront.

Sooner or later business leaders must make decisions that people in the company may experience as inconsistent with their earlier emphasis on "one big happy family." Once decisions get made that run counter to someone's personal desires, it is all too easy for people to think that these leaders didn't mean it when they talked about their commitment to people and wanting them to be content in their work.

"How could he make me work weekends?" asked one banking employee. "He knows that's when I play softball. All this talk about supporting people in having time for their personal life." This person's boss does want people to have a personal life, but in order to be competitive, the bank has to be open more than five days a week. Expanding the bank's hours meant people were going to have to work Saturdays on a rotating schedule.

"I didn't get the transfer I wanted," complained an employee in an advertising company. "My manager keeps talking about promoting people from within the organization. She's just saying that to sound good." The person who said this did not have the skills needed to do the job he wanted. The owner had no choice but to hire someone else for the job, even though she knew that this particular employee badly wanted to be considered for the position. He was considered, but he simply did not make the cut.

Basing working relationships on close personal ties can lead people to believe that leaders will base their decisions on what people want or hope for rather than what might be best for the business. When they then make decisions that are based on business considerations, some people feel personally betrayed. It is almost as if a parent has broken a promise. This is the corporate version of "If you really loved me, you would give me what I want." Lacking a clear understanding of the difference between what is personal and what is professional at work, it is too easy for people to end up feeling like the basic promises of the relationship have not been kept. Or worse yet, they may reach the conclusion that the leader's emphasis on close personal ties was all a sham to begin with—it was all a ploy to get more out of people.

Co-workers end up with the same problems with each other when working together is based on personal feelings. Suppose you and I work together on the same project and I am doing something that is intruding on your effectiveness. What will happen to our warm feelings if you raise this issue with me, particularly if the topic is one that I may not be open to hearing? You may, for example, think that I have not been doing my job properly. I may have been failing to do something that you were expecting me to do, or I may have treated a customer in a way that is not consistent with the company's values.

What will happen to our relationship if you bring this issue to my attention? Will I be angry with you? Will I be so personally offended that I end up sulking around the office, making it clear to everyone that I am upset and that you had better not bother me with anything else that day? Will our relationship be damaged, making it all the more difficult for us to work together in the coming days?

When people overemphasize close personal feelings as the basis of teamwork and leadership, it can create an environment that feels good to everyone involved—until some problem arises that causes conflict. The very thought of raising issues for discussion can feel so threatening to our relationship that problems end up going underground. Warm, cozy relationships at work can be so tenuous that even mild conflicts can be seen as too dangerous to talk about. The end result is silence, with unresolved problems damaging effectiveness and morale.

If we base our working relationships on **friendship,** we will almost certainly have **problems** dealing with **conflict.**

"I Don't Have to Be Liked—I Just Want to Be Respected"

Sometimes I hear leaders and team members take the exact opposite stance on relationships at work. Some try to skirt the issue, stating that they are here to work, not to be liked or to make friends. They believe that you cannot be close to people and manage them effectively. They keep their distance, making sure that they don't get too close to the people on their team.

Others go so far as to assert that they don't care what others think of them; they just want to be respected. When leaders state the need for respect in such strong terms, they almost inevitably turn out to be the kind of people I would never want to work with, or for. Their stance on "respect" is often just a justification for being a tyrant as a manager. They are remote and unknowable, putting no effort into getting to know the people who work for them. They typically invest little effort in coaching. If they comment on performance at all, you can be assured that it will be negative and critical. Praise or appreciation will be all but nonexistent. The people on their team fear them, finding them to be overly critical and impossible to please. Being feared should never be confused with being respected. Respect must be earned, and it requires a level of admiration and esteem for the person who is respected. Intimidating, personally remote leaders do not deserve respect. They haven't earned it.

People who insist on respect rarely get it.

Different Purposes, Different Rules

A professional relationship exists solely for the purpose of getting work accomplished. The purpose of personal relationships is to develop a form of personal connection between people. Confusion about the difference between personal and professional relationships is responsible for many of the difficulties we face in the workplace today. Our inability to see these two relationships clearly and to know how to make each of these relationships work with our co-workers undermines teamwork, ruins personal job satisfaction, and damages people's success on the job.

We can have a wide variety of personal relationships at work, ranging from casual acquaintanceships to close friendship and love relationships. In these relationships we find many things that meet our needs. However, it is important for us to remember that the primary purpose of our relationships at work is to get a job done. We may work with or for someone we come to regard as a friend. We need to keep reminding ourselves that the topic of most of our conversations is not personal—it is professional. This is especially true in times of disagreement about work. What is going on between us has nothing to do with how we feel about each other. It is about getting the job done.

Personal Choice

In personal relationships, personal choice is involved. If I do not like someone, I can choose not to have that person in my life. If I make a new acquaintance and find that I like that person, I can act to increase the amount of intimacy between the two of us. The other person, of course, can decide to decline my request to deepen the relationship. That is the nature of personal relationships—they exist to the degree that both parties involved are willing. Each of us has a choice.

There is little personal choice involved in professional relationships. You probably did not choose your co-workers or your boss. You took a job and found yourself becoming a part of what might turn out to be a very strange cast of characters. You are almost certain, at different points in your career, to have co-workers you would never choose to have as friends. You will find yourself working with people with whom you seem to have absolutely nothing in common. You may disagree about political or social issues. Your ages may be very different, leaving you with very different preferences in music or weekend activities. Some may turn out to be people you just do not like, who seem to have few, if any, redeeming qualities to speak of.

Nevertheless, if you are on the same team, you need to find a way to work together. Neither of you has any choice in the matter. The company needs the skills that each of you brings to the team and expects you to be able to work together, whether you like each other personally or not. While you can cut off a personal relationship if the other person does not suit you, you cannot cut off a professional relationship with a co-worker if the demands of the job require you to work together. Remember, in a professional relationship *your feelings about the other person are not relevant*. There is a job to be done. That is why you are in a relationship in the first place.

> **Liking** everyone you work with is **not a requirement.** It is not even a **reasonable expectation.**

Power Dynamics

In personal relationships, there is an assumption of equality in the relationship. Neither of us, at least ideally, should be any more or less powerful than the other.

Professional relationships, by their very nature, include establishing clarity about the degree of power each person has relative to the other person. And differences in power can add unforeseen complications to what at one time may have been a very satisfying personal relationship.

While on a consulting project in a manufacturing facility, I was talking with a woman who had recently been promoted to supervisor. She was now leading the team she had been a member of for several years. She talked about the difficult time she was having with the impact of her promotion on her relationship with the rest of the team:

I have known these people for a long time. We have worked together and partied together. But everything has changed since I became the supervisor. I thought people would be happy to get someone they already knew as the new supervisor. Yet everyone is resentful of me now. They don't seem to be as comfortable with me as they used to be. I just didn't expect things to change so much, and I don't like it at all.

We talked for a while, exploring the differences between personal and professional relationships. When one person in a peer group gets promoted to lead that group, the group's professional relationships are redefined by a change in power. One person, who used to be a fellow team member, now has the responsibility and authority to lead the team and hold people accountable for their performance. People suddenly find themselves getting instructions and job assignments from someone they have long considered a friend and an equal. This can be a difficult adjustment for some people, leaving them wanting to distance themselves from their old friend/new supervisor. As a result, the ease and comfort of the personal relationships sometimes suffer.

We decided that the best thing for the new supervisor to do would be to talk about this with those employees who were having trouble with her promotion. She met with them individually and acknowledged that this had been a tough transition for them and for her. She wanted them to know that she recognized that there had been a significant change in their professional relationship. It was now her job to attend management meetings and bring back information and directions to the team. It was also her job to pay attention to their performance and provide coaching when she felt it might be helpful. Here is what she told them:

I've tried putting myself in your shoes and I wondered how I would react if you were now my supervisor. You know what? I would probably have some trouble with the change in our relationship, too. This is not an easy shift for us to make. But I want to promise you that I will do my best to represent this team's needs with upper management. I also want to be the best supervisor I can be, and if you think there is anything I can do to do that job better, I want you to let me know.

We have been friends for a long time. I hope that you will continue to think of me as a friend. The change in our roles here at work isn't personal. It is professional, and it involves a shift in our working relationship with each other. I still think of you as my friend and I would like for us to be able to maintain our friendship in spite of the changes that have happened here at work.

In visiting with her later, she told me that it had gone very well with two out of three conversations. She felt connected to those two friends once again. Just giving them a chance to talk about things and to separate out the personal from the professional seemed to help them think about the situation more clearly. The other person is still keeping her distance interpersonally. The new supervisor was willing to accept this as one of the unfortunate outcomes of an otherwise positive change in her career development.

Different Methods of Communication

It is possible to have both personal and professional relationships with the same people at work. To do this successfully, we have to remember that the differing purposes of these two relationships require different methods of communicating with the same people. This can only work if each of us understands, moment by moment, whether we are relating to each other personally or professionally.

Personal relationships provide support, intimacy, sharing, and companionship. The level of intimacy we have with a particular person shapes communications within personal relationships. Some relationships are quite casual and limited to small talk—we tell jokes or talk about our weekend and anything else that we might have in common. But the more intimacy and support we want from any given relationship, the more intimate and personal our conversations. Since the purpose of personal relationships is to establish some level of intimacy with the other person, our communications are driven by that desire and reflect our intent.

Consider what happens when a significant relationship issue arises between you and someone you feel very close to. If your intent is to talk about this issue in order to feel closer to the other person, then it will be very appropriate to talk about your feelings. In personal relationships, how you feel about something is important to the other person. Talking about your feelings with the other person is healthy and appropriate, given the level of intimacy between the two of you.

However, in our professional relationship with the same person, the rules change. The purpose of your conversations is to get a job done, not to build intimacy. In fact, you may not even *desire* any level of intimacy with the other person. A cordial, professional relationship will sometimes do well enough. When relating to each other in our professional roles, the focus of our conversations needs to be on, and stay on, the job.

I am now going to present a very important point: sometimes your personal feelings are not relevant in a conversation about work. In fact, sometimes your feelings about some situation at work are not only irrelevant, they may also be dangerous to talk about.

Nothing complicates **conflict** resolution **faster than** "sharing your **feelings."**

We will thoroughly explore this topic in the rest of the book. For now, I want you to understand that one of the most important skills for co-workers to develop is to know how to keep conversations on track and in the "right mode." Sometimes we need to remind each other and ourselves that there is nothing personal going on here. There is a job to get done. By this I do not mean that your personal feelings about your work are not important. Of course they are. I hope that you bring a great deal of personal passion and commitment to your work. It is just that it sometimes helps us get things done if we put our personal feelings to the side for a while. We will talk about this throughout the book.

When the Business Is the Family

It is a pleasure to own a business that is successful and that puts the owner in the position of being able to bring sons, daughters, and other relatives into the family business. This creates complications, however, for the rest of the company, who then work with those family members. Suppose, for example, you work with the owner's son or daughter. You can't help but wonder how far to take it when you have a conflict with that person. If you manage family members, you may have concerns about how to intervene if there are any serious performance issues to be dealt with. This can be made to work, but only if it is clear to everyone that family members are to be treated no differently than anyone else on the team. This sounds good in theory but is difficult to put into practice.

The family-owned business presents some of the greatest challenges in keeping personal and professional issues straight. When husbands work with wives, when parents employ their sons and daughters, or when any other combination of relatives work in the same company, there is much room for confusion. The case studies on pages 22 to 24 are some examples from my own consulting experience.

Having It All

Mixing personal and professional relationships at work can be confusing. Sometimes it is even difficult. But I don't want to be misunderstood. I am not saying that it is either undesirable or impossible to have both kinds of relationships between team members and between management and staff. But I have come to believe that this is possible only when the following steps are taken:

- First, everyone involved must understand the difference between personal and professional relationships.
- Second, everyone involved must learn how to communicate appropriately when relating to each other in their professional roles.
- Third, everyone must collaborate to accomplish their mission as an organization.

Collaboration must include the kind of wide-open communication in which people can openly disagree with one another and with management, identify problems and solve them, and experiment with new, more efficient ways of getting things done. A hallmark of collaboration, especially in times of conflict, should be: "Nothing personal; there's a job to get done."

Once we have collaboration and open, professional communication, then we have the luxury of focusing on developing close, personal connections with those we work with. First, it will be easier to build personal relationships when we know that we can work powerfully together and disagree without taking things personally. In addition, we will find that the other people are in fact more attractive to us personally once we have discovered we can work together. It is simply easier to like people when we are able to work out the mechanics of working together.

Case Studies in the Ultimate Mix of Relationships at Work

No One Is Speaking to Anyone

The owner of a small family firm that was at risk of going out of business had recently demoted his son. He had then promoted his son's wife into the son's former position! It would be an understatement for me to say that there was tension in the office. My own assessment of the situation was that the father had done exactly the right thing. His daughter-in-law, it turned out, had the skills and temperament to do the job very well. The son, on the other hand, not only was ineffective at the job, but he didn't like it. He had even considered quitting before all this had happened. But having his father demote him was a blow to his ego. He had all but stopped speaking to his father, and things were more than a little cool between his wife and him.

The "fix" turned out to be surprisingly simple. They needed an outsider like myself to confirm that everything was as it should be for the business. They all needed to be reminded as well that family is family and business is business. They needed to reaffirm their caring for each other, all the while acknowledging that the father had had no choice but to take action and put his son into a role that was better suited to his talents, doing work that he actually liked.

The Quest for Succession

Two brothers, who were soon due to retire, owned together a thriving business that they had established and developed. Each brother had two sons. All four sons had been part of the business for years, and one brother from each pair had expressed a strong desire to be the next president. I was asked to assess which of the four, if any, had the qualities to make a good president and then determine if the other three were willing to support that person. Barring that, the founders were going to sell the business.

The brothers who had founded the business were very clear about the need to separate personal from professional considerations. While each would have liked one of his sons to take over the leadership role, they also knew that the decision could not be based on personal preferences.

One of them put it this way:

This is business. We have spent years building this company and we have no intention of seeing our legacy waste away because we did not have the courage to sell the company in order to save it. We employ nearly three hundred people here. We are not about to put their families at risk by turning this business over to someone who is not suited to lead it. My sons and nephews might not like it, but that is the way it is going to be.

I admired this man's clarity of thinking and his willingness to put his own wishes aside for the sake of the whole, especially since he felt one of his own sons was best suited for the role.

In my judgment, neither of the cousins who wanted the job so badly was even remotely qualified. The one who was most suited to the job was the least likely, on the face of it. He was the youngest of the four. He was also the most self-effacing. But his heart and soul were in the business and, though only in his early thirties, he had already demonstrated real promise as a leader. After a family council, the group fully endorsed him to be groomed as the next president. They created a five-year technical and leadership development program, gearing him up to become president when the brothers retired. Ten years have passed, and both the company and the family relationships are doing very well.

Working with the Boss's Son

I once consulted to a family-owned business that was suffering some morale problems that were hard for the owner to understand. I found that his son was the topic of many of the team's complaints. Ron, we'll call him, loved to throw his weight around. It was not uncommon for him to walk up to managers and tell them what to do. Some of them learned to ignore it and accept it as one of the unfortunate aspects of an otherwise good job. Managers who were less sure of themselves felt put on the spot in that they did not want to alienate the person who might one day run the company. Nor did they feel comfortable going to their boss, Ron's father, to discuss an uncomfortable situation.

Ron had an even greater impact on nonmanagement employees. He would tell people what to do, and his "directions" sometimes ran counter to the instructions they had received from their own manager. What, they thought, were they to do? Ron would go so far as to remind them that his name was Smith and that they had better watch out because they would be working for him someday.

I would like to be able to tell you that I managed to pull off a wonderful consulting intervention in this project. I didn't. The owner was not willing to hear any information that suggested that his boy was anything less than perfect. He felt that the people I had talked to were jealous of Ron. He went on to say that Ron had always been a little difficult to handle, but that he was basically a "good boy." (Ron was in his thirties at the time.) He promised to give the matter some thought and said we would talk the following week to plan next steps. Unfortunately, that was the end of it. He never returned another one of my calls.

You may be wondering, "Why not leave well enough alone? Once people learn how to work together, shouldn't that be enough? After all, aren't they paid to work together? Should companies put energy into building cultures in which people work together and, at the same time, are able to connect with each other personally as well?"

First things first: build **open** and **effective** professional **relationships,** and **personal** relationships **will follow.**

The answer is yes, for at least two reasons. First, while personal and professional relationships can be thought of as two distinctly different relationships, when we like each other, it supports our professional relationship. It is easier to work with people if we feel connected to them personally. It is certainly easier to get through conflicts and maintain trust if we have a personal bond that helps us stay in communication with each other.

There is another, equally significant, reason. People who like their job and their co-workers are more likely to stay with the company. Many companies are finding it increasingly difficult to find and retain qualified staff. Once they find good people, they want to keep them. That is why companies are experimenting with so many new ways of doing business, ranging from on-site day care for children to flextime.

One approach companies can take is to pay more attention to the quality of the culture of their organization. Some companies commit themselves to building an organization that is a great place to work. They know that if people are able to be productive while working with people they like and feel connected with personally, they are much more likely to find satisfaction in their work.

Building personal relationships is just as important to you as an individual. While I will continue to emphasize the importance of attending to your professional relationships first, we will also be talking about things you can do to build trust and closer personal relationships at work. You want to be able to build the kinds of interpersonal connections with people at work that enable you to create mutual support and comradeship with your teammates. You will also find that the more you are able to get people to be comfortable with you and like you, the more successful you will be in your career. The following exercise will help you assess the qualities you want to bring into your relationships at work.

We will be returning to the topic of personal development, especially in the last section of the book. If your reflection on these exercises leaves you feeling like you have a lot of work to do, don't despair. There is

Exercise 5
Identifying Qualities for Balancing Personal and Professional Relationships

Think back over your work history. Identify someone in a leadership position who was able to relate to people with personal warmth and affection while operating effectively as a leader. That is, this person was able to offer corrective coaching when it was needed and to make hard decisions, yet still managed to maintain a close relationship with the people he or she led.

• List as many qualities as you can that made this person such a special person to work for. See if you can identify some of the things that made it possible for him or her to feel close

to his or her people without this closeness limiting his or her effectiveness as a leader.

After listing these personal characteristics, reflect on the following questions:

• Imagine I were to ask your co-workers (or your team, if you are a leader) how you rate on the characteristics you identified above. On which qualities are you close to being the kind of person you want to be?

• Where are you falling short of your own ideals for the kind of person you would like to be as a co-worker?

• Identify two or three action steps that could help you make some improvements in exhibiting those qualities. A magical transformation is not expected. Lasting character change comes with small steps and practice.

much you can do, and none of it has to be all that complicated. Identifying simple things to do is easy. Finding the commitment and courage to act can be challenging, but it is easier to consider acting if giant steps are not required.

Chapter Three

When Good Teams Go Bad

Years ago I was working on a consulting project involving a team that was dealing with conflict and confusion regarding how they were going to work together. In reviewing my findings with the president, it struck me that it was almost as if I were looking down into a box, looking at a group of dedicated people working very hard to get the job done. Unfortunately, they were all pushing on different walls of the box, and it was very hard for them to get the box to move in one direction.

Yet when I talked to them, all they wanted was to work on a team where everyone was pushing on the same wall of the box. (Note to engineers who may have trouble with this analogy, arguing that the box has a floor in it, so pushing on the walls to make the box move doesn't make any sense—it's just a metaphor, OK?)

Pushing on different walls of the box is hard on the people inside the box. It takes a lot of effort to get anything done when your teammates seem to be going in different directions. If people work in this condition for a long period of time, it can be stressful and discouraging. After a while, they may just quit caring. After all, why should they keep working so hard when it takes so much effort to get something done?

Pushing on different walls of the box is costly to the organization as well. The team's uncoordinated effort affects their efficiency, reduces the quality of their work, and adds to the cost of their products and services. When people push on different walls of the box, everyone loses.

Every company has times when people are pushing on different walls of the box. Sometimes this happens within a single team. Sometimes different teams within the same company seem to be going in different directions. The following exercise will help you identify examples of times when people on your team are pushing on different walls of the box.

Exercise 6
Where Are People Going in Different Directions in Your Company?

- List at least three examples where you see people in your company pushing on different walls of the box.

- How does this uncoordinated effort affect the company?

- How is it affecting quality and your company's service to its customers?

- What is the impact on you personally when you come to work and try to get things done but others seem to have something else in mind?

Teamwork Doesn't Come Naturally

Why is it that so many teams wind up, at least occasionally, pushing on different walls of the box? The answer to this question lies in a flawed assumption that we make about work that can set us up for trouble—"Teamwork should come naturally."

I've come to believe that businesses are prone to making this mistaken assumption when it comes to building a staff to run their business. Most companies screen job applicants very carefully. They are sure to hire people with the right training and experience. They also try to hire people with good character and personal integrity. Once employees are hired, business owners do their best to provide them with the resources needed to get the job done. They also try to provide them with an environment that is both pleasant to work in and appropriate for the nature of the work being done. Then they stand back and ask people to work together.

When people start pushing on different walls of the box, their leaders begin to wonder, "What is going on here? These are good people. They have the skills and resources to get the job done. Why can't they work together?"

If you think about it for a moment, you can understand these leaders' frustration. It looks to them like everything should be in place for their company to work very well—good people, proper resources, a good working environment. But instead of asking why people can't seem to work together, I think a better question to consider is, "Why do we think people *should* know how to work together?"

Working together doesn't come easily. In spite of their best efforts, people with good intentions all too often end up pushing on different walls of the box. In America, the words "teamwork" and "team player" are almost cultural clichés. Most of us have been hearing about teamwork since we were children. People in job interviews are asked about their strengths, and a standard answer is to proclaim oneself a "team player." But it takes more than good intentions for people to be able to work together effectively. It requires the interpersonal skills necessary for working with other people.

No matter what you do, you must master a body of technical skills, learned on or off the job, to do your job well. But if you are going to be truly successful at work, focusing solely on your technical abilities will not be enough. It will be just as important for you to be constantly developing your ability to work with and through other people. It is hard to imagine a job that doesn't require the ability to work with other people. While there may be a few jobs that require very little interaction with other people, most jobs today require ongoing interaction with co-workers and managers. Some jobs also require intensive work with customers or with the people from other companies who provide the goods and services needed for your company to stay in business.

Filling a room with team players **does not guarantee teamwork.**

Everyone would agree that interpersonal abilities are important to our success at work. But think about your training for a moment. Most of the training you received probably focused on the technical side of your work. Communication training is often reserved for those who have contact with customers. Companies recognize that customer service can be demanding and can tax the good intentions of even the most dedicated worker. Yet many companies seem to assume that their staff will just naturally know how to build good working relationships with their co-workers, that they will know how to identify problems and resolve the conflicts that inevitably occur when people work together.

The good news is that most of us do pretty well with teamwork most of the time. Unfortunately, there are times when we don't seem to be able to make things work with other people on the job. Circumstances make teamwork all the more challenging. Change at work puts stress on people. Heavy workloads and long hours result in tired, frustrated people who sometimes say things they wouldn't normally say. We may be assigned to work with a co-worker who is hard to get along with or we may get a new boss who is impossible to please. Sooner or later, we are all confronted with interpersonal situations that are almost impossible for us to deal with effectively.

Personalizing Conflict Is the First Step in Relationship Breakdown

Knowing how to build teamwork and collaboration with co-workers is the foundation for effective working relationships. Our entry point into this conversation about teamwork will be conflict. Conflict at work can be terribly disruptive. Poorly managed, conflict kills teamwork, undermines trust between co-workers, and damages companies and the public they serve. In extreme cases, some people handle conflicts so poorly that they end up damaging their careers.

Conflict, properly managed, **seeds growth, creativity,** and **change.**

Conflict itself is not the problem. When people are put together in teams and asked to accomplish something by working together, conflict is not only predictable, it is inevitable. In fact, conflict can even be seen as *desirable*. If you are lucky, you work on a team where people can openly disagree with each other and argue for differing points of view. That is how teams get smarter and are able to take advantage of the collective intelligence of the group. The problem is not conflict itself but, rather, how we *experience* it.

When we are involved in a conflict at work, it's only natural for us to want to explain the situation to ourselves so that we can understand it and deal with it. Let's imagine that I am consulting the company you work for. As I always do, I will be spending time on site where you work, talking to people about the company and how they feel about working there. In the course of my assessment, I have a conversation with you and you tell me about a conflict you are having with a co-worker. Let's call him Fred.

One of my questions to you is, "Why are you in conflict? What is the source of the problem?" If you are like most people I've asked this question to, you will *know* with absolute certainty why you are in conflict: "I am working with a *jerk!*" When we are in conflict, we usually point our finger at the other person.

"But what is it about the other person that is causing the problem?" I then ask. The answer I most frequently get is that the conflict can best be understood as a personality problem—and rarely do we think it's *our* personality that is at fault. We almost always think that this "personality conflict" is attributable to the personality, character, or intentions of other people. They are behaving the way they do because they are "jerks." Anyone can see that. It is perfectly obvious.

Flawed Conflict Diagnosis #1: The personality of the other person.

Jerk, as we are using it here, is a technical term. We have many ways of describing *jerkness.* In our conversation about Fred, you might describe him as "arrogant," "overbearing," "turf building," "uncooperative," "aggressive," or "selfish." The list of destructive terms I've heard people use to describe their bosses, peers, and staff could go on to fill this page. As I am sure you can imagine, some of the terms I've heard wouldn't be appropriate to include here.

After talking to you, I decide to spend time with Fred. Our conversation reveals that he has a much less emotional way of sorting out the problem the two of you are having with each other. He knows that you are a good person, that you are a loving parent to your children, and that you do good service in your community. He does not feel that the problem should be attributed to personality—yours or his. He trusts that you are a good person and that you probably have good intentions.

Flawed Conflict Diagnosis #2: Incompetence of the other person.

But Fred does have an explanation for the conflict. While he hasn't reached the conclusion that you are a jerk, he does have a way of understanding the situation that is as destructive as your conclusion that he is a jerk. He, too, is pointing at the other person as being the source of the problem. Right now, he believes he is having a problem working with you because you are incompetent! You just don't have the intelligence, ability, or training necessary for you to do your job, at least not with regard to the particular issue over which the two of you are in conflict.

There you have it. When teamwork breaks down and we find ourselves in conflict with one of our teammates, we have a tendency to blame the problem on the personality or incompetence of the other person. Once we have sized up the situation in this way, resolving the problem looks next to impossible. After all, how do you approach someone about a problem when you believe that the problem resides in the personality or capabilities of the other person involved?

The Problem with Explosive Conflict

When we diagnose a conflict as residing in the personality or incompetence of the other person, we have already created the foundation for an explosive conversation. Suppose someone approaches you to tell you what a complete jerk she thinks you are. She probably won't use that term, but she will use other descriptive terms that are not easy for you to hear. She may describe you as only interested in your own agenda and lacking the cooperative spirit of a good team player. She may accuse you of failing to keep your agreements, of not caring about other people, and of not being trustworthy.

It may have taken her a week to get up the nerve to talk to you about this. Sometimes raising a difficult issue for discussion is an act of personal courage or, at least, desperation. While her intentions may be good, this conversation is likely to spiral out of control. I don't know about you, but if someone approaches me to talk about what a jerk he thinks I am, I will probably go to great pains to *prove* it to him: "So you think I'm a jerk. I am sorry, but you seem to have confused me with someone who cares what you think!"

Herein lies the trap: Talking about your assessment of the other person's intentions or capabilities is a fast track to a defensive reaction. When people feel like they are being personally attacked, their natural response is to defend themselves. When they do, you will probably try to provide more examples of what you mean, only this time you will make your points a bit louder and more emotionally. Pretty soon the conversation turns into a full-blown argument.

This is especially true when the person raising the issue has a full head of emotional steam going into the conversation. We may have thought about this problem for a long time, trying to get up the courage to talk about it. When the other person fails to listen and starts to defend herself, it is very easy for emotions to take control. We wind up saying things we later regret saying. We may even indulge ourselves in the satisfaction of telling the other person how we really feel about her. Some conversations get so heated that the relationship between the two people involved ends up in far worse shape than it was before the conversation started. Damage has been done. Later, reflecting on the conversation, we will realize that in the heat of battle, we forgot to say all the things we could have said that might have had this conversation end on a more positive note. We have had yet another lesson in the danger of speaking our mind. Next time, we may be more cautious and not speak up at all.

Most of us have had times when our emotions got out of control and damaged a relationship or, at the very least, left us feeling a bit sheepish about our own behavior. The exercise below will help you avoid this by being aware of your actions and their potential for damage.

Emotions unleashed almost always **do more damage** to the **sender** than they do to the **receiver.**

Silence Is Deadly

The collusion of silence happens at many levels. Sometimes it is just between two people. One of them may have deeply held feelings about the other but not talk about them for fear of the outcome. Sometimes it is between management and the people who work for them. Management may profess a commitment to open doors and participatory decision making. The people who work for them may feel that in reality their opinions mean nothing and disagreements are suppressed. Yet when management speaks in glowing terms about their corporate values of

Exercise 7
Avoiding the Foot in the Mouth

• Describe a time when you wound up saying things you wish you hadn't said.

• What was the impact on your relationship with the other person?

• How did this affect your ability to work with him or her?

• What have you done as a result of these kinds of incidents? Did you learn to speak up more appropriately? Did you make a decision to just keep your mouth shut?

Some opinions are endlessly discussed . . . with everyone but the people who need to hear them.

participation and involvement, no one will stand up and say anything to the contrary. Sure, they will complain to each other and roll their eyes when a senior manager talks about how "our people are our most important asset." But does it get talked about in a way that will make any difference? Not likely.

It's the Unspoken Words That Kill Relationships

When talking to people about conflicts, I always ask, "Have you talked to him about this?" The answer is often, "Are you crazy? I can't talk to him about *that!*" A conversation I had with Janice, a supervisor in a manufacturing environment, is typical. She was describing one of the other supervisors, Ted, who was creating problems for the rest of the team. She described Ted as the dominating force on the team. In staff meetings, he was loud, aggressive, and domineering. Physically, he could be very intimidating. He is well over six feet tall and very muscular. At times, she said, he "gets in your face, standing over you and making his point with a finger pointing at your chest."

I asked how their team meetings went. Janice told me that the rest of the team had convinced the manager to stop having them. She described the manager as being weak and unable to deal with Ted's aggressive style, and the rest of the supervisory team as being so intimidated by Ted that there was very little open discussion in the meetings. Ted would always do most of the talking and, over time, his opinion prevailed in most discussions. The rest of the team felt that continuing to hold these meetings was a frustrating waste of time.

When I asked Janice about approaching Ted to talk about this, she rolled her eyes and said, "Right. Like *that* will make any difference. *You* work with him for a while. Then come back and tell me how things are designed to work if only people would talk to each other." The rest of the team shared her opinion. The situation looked too difficult to talk about, so the problem was going on unaddressed and unresolved. Why raise an issue if you believe it will only result in more conflict?

I then talked to Ted about the perceptions that others on the team had shared with me. What I said to him took him by surprise. While he knew that he put people off a bit, he was unaware of the seriousness of the impact he was having on the people around him. For one thing, his physical size was something that was working against him. Most of his co-workers, especially the women, were much smaller than he was. They also worked in a noisy environment. When they talked, they needed to get close and speak loudly. Ted was coming across as intimidating, when sometimes all he wanted was to be heard over the machinery.

He was also distressed to hear that his abrupt manner of speaking and his tendency to speak his mind freely were creating problems in team meetings. He was assertive and unafraid of conflict and made the mistake of assuming that everyone else was as comfortable with disagreement as he was. He respected people who took him on, and when they didn't, he just assumed they agreed with him. It hadn't occurred to him that his verbal style had managed to quash open discussion in team meetings. While he certainly needed coaching on how to encourage open communication, Ted was anything but the overbearing jerk everyone thought him to be. Unfortunately, his teammates had drawn so many damaging conclusions about his personality that approaching him to talk about the problem seemed pointless, if not downright dangerous. The damage had been done to the relationship.

Nothing kills relationships more surely than issues left unspoken.

Pockets of silence occur in every organization. Issues persist because people aren't willing to talk about them. For example, you may have a manager who is ineffective in some way that is obvious to everyone but him or her. Yet no one starts the conversation that might make a difference. The following exercise will help you get in touch with the costs of silence.

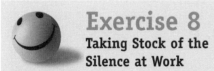

Exercise 8
Taking Stock of the Silence at Work

- List at least three issues affecting you, your team, or your company as a whole that persist because people aren't talking about them.

- What keeps people from bringing these issues to the table for discussion?

- What impact are these issues having on you?

- On your co-workers?

- On your company and the customers you serve?

The Rhinoceros Head in the Corner

Silence about certain topics becomes the operating principle in some organizations. It's as if I walk into an office and notice that over in the corner of the room there is a rhinoceros head. Someone has spread a tablecloth on it and managed to balance a lamp on the horn. Everyone ignores it and acts as if it's a table. No one says, "Look at that. There is a rhinoceros head in the corner. Isn't this a bit odd? Why is it that we have a rhinoceros head in the corner and no one is talking about it?"

Silence is killing our organizations.

Many issues in organizations occur between groups such as departments or teams. Problems in coordinating efforts with other units often get personalized, with members of the group involved personalizing the problem. Only this time, they aren't thinking about individuals as much as about entire groups, with thoughts like, "Those people in accounting don't care what goes on out here on the shop floor." Or, "Salespeople are just order takers. They don't even bother to find out what the customer actually needs, and then they make commitments we can't possibly keep." The following case study is an example of this.

Exercise 9 will help you identify opportunities to open up communication across department or team boundaries.

Exercise 9
Communicating Across Department Lines

- Identify an issue that crosses team boundaries and is having a serious impact on your work group.
- Describe what is going on.

- How is the problem being personalized? What are people in your unit saying about the other team?
- What issues are you avoiding talking about?
- What barriers are keeping the two groups from getting together to talk about and resolve this issue?

Case Study of Lack of Communication Across Department Lines

I once led a team development session for the claims department of an insurance company. One of their jobs was to resolve claims problems, some of which were caused by mistakes made by the department that entered the claims into the system. They started talking about the jerks and incompetents over in that department. People were saying things like: "They don't even care about service over there. All they want to do is get on to the next claim." "They obviously don't understand how the system is supposed to work. Anyone with half a brain could see how they are screwing up on claims entries." "All they care about is numbers. All they want to do is get a lot of claims into the system without a thought about the quality of their work."

The conversation was starting to turn into a feeding frenzy when one brave young woman in the back of the room raised her hand to speak. "I just transferred over here from the entry department. I want you to know that they are saying a lot of similar things about people over here in claims." As the discussion continued, the group discovered that the entry department was just as concerned about quality as they were but that they were under enormous pressure, trying to catch up with a huge backlog of claims to be entered. Moreover, the newly transferred person was starting to see how technical problems in the entry system were resulting in unintended errors that later had to be cleaned up by the claims staff.

The people in both departments wanted to do a good job. Nevertheless, the claims people reduced problems in entry to the "carelessness" and "lack of commitment" of the other team. When I asked if the two groups had ever sat down to talk about this, the answer was predictably negative. They were just doing the best they could to work with the claims generated by a team that obviously, as they saw it, didn't care about the quality of their work. Again, silence was taking its toll.

Chapter Four

When Behavior Falls Short of Good Intentions

Wouldn't it be nice if you could go to work, do your job, and enjoy yourself in the process? After all, that is all most of us want—meaningful work done in an environment that adds to the quality of our working life. And that is what most companies will tell you they are trying to provide. But intention is one thing. Reality is all too often something else.

Those "Problem People"

All it takes is one person to ruin what might otherwise be a very good job. That person might be your boss. Or perhaps you have a co-worker who seems to be intent on making your life miserable. We have all experienced this at some point in our careers. Learning to understand and work with such "problem people" may be one of the most important survival skills for you to develop. Let's see if some of the following examples sound familiar.

"A Good Day Is a Day I Haven't Had to Talk to My Boss"

Raoul is a senior vice president in a manufacturing firm. In many ways, he is typical of some of the hard-driving executives you'll find in almost any kind of company. He is one of the best professionals in the company. He has a reputation for hard work, long hours, and a passionate commitment to serving the needs of his customers.

He works for a company that provides manufacturing equipment and on-site service for its customers. It does business in a highly competitive market. If it doesn't respond quickly, there are plenty of competitors waiting to take its customers away. Speed and good customer relations are essential.

If the only measure of Raoul's success were his dealings with customers, he would be a company president's dream. His customers love him. Raoul is willing to do whatever it takes to meet their needs, solve their problems, and keep their manufacturing lines up and running. His customers know that if they call him, he will produce results. They also like him personally. He is highly intelligent and has a demonstrated grasp of his products and his customers' manufacturing processes. He develops relationships with customers with the same passion he brings to the rest of his work. He stays in touch with them by phone, and when he is in their area, they can count on him stopping by for coffee and a conversation about how things are going. One of the reasons they stick with him and his company is their assurance that he understands them and their needs.

Raoul's commitment to the customer, paired with his demonstrated technical expertise, leaves many people predicting that he will be the next president of the company when the current president retires in a few years. His future is very bright. What makes him all the more unusual is that he is such a young man. He is barely out of his thirties. Clearly, Raoul has a great future in front of him.

There is, however, one major problem that may have an impact on Raoul's career. As much as people outside the company love him, I heard very different perceptions about Raoul from people within the company. His peers universally respect him. They see the quality of the job he is doing and its impact on the continued growth of the company. At the same time, many of them told me that they probably wouldn't like working for him. Why? "Well, I hear from my staff that he's a tyrant."

The magic words "please" and "thank you" still go a long way.

Interviews with his staff confirmed what Raoul's peers had heard about him. While they all respected his drive and his results, many of them could not stand working for him. He produced results, but did so by relentlessly pushing his staff, regardless of the costs to them personally. Yet the long hours and the hard work didn't bother people as much as how he treated them, as one person expressed:

Raoul never asks you to do anything. It is always a command. There are so many times when I would obviously be willing to do what needs to be done, but he doesn't have to order me around. It is so belittling. Why doesn't he have the courtesy to ask?

As you might expect from someone who demands so much of himself, Raoul sets equally high standards for his staff, and he is none too gentle in dealing with problems in performance. "When Raoul is upset about something," explained another person, "everyone knows about it."

He looks angry. His face gets red. I feel like hiding under my desk when I see him coming my way. Last week I missed a deadline. He crucified me in the staff meeting. The truth is I screwed up and had it coming. But it was so embarrassing to get such a strongly worded chewing out right there in front of the rest of the team. Why couldn't he have talked to me privately after the meeting?

A meeting isn't the only arena for a public dressing-down. His service personnel carry radios. It is not at all uncommon for Raoul to get upset about something and then get on the radio and give someone a bad time. While using the radio to communicate is fast and efficient, everyone who is carrying a radio at the time can't help but overhear the conversation. It is another public embarrassment for the target of Raoul's anger.

Even the paging system within their building can be a source of public humiliation, said another:

Raoul has a way of paging someone to his office that lets everyone in the building know who is in trouble. It isn't what he says as much as it is his tone of voice. The last time he paged me like that I felt like everyone was watching me as I walked to his office.

Not everyone is intimidated by Raoul's aggressive style. One person commented:

I've learned that you have to stand up to Raoul. He likes people who are just as aggressive as he is. You can go into his office, close the door, and have it out with him. But you had better know what you are talking about. I'm careful to make sure that I know exactly what I am talking about and that all my facts are straight. If I don't, he can be pretty hard to take at times.

Some people noted the same need for fearlessness in meetings:

Raoul can be pretty intimidating in a meeting, but he will listen if you stand up for yourself. You have to be willing to disagree with him. If you don't prove your case, he won't hesitate to point it out in front of everyone. The problem is that he scares a lot of people so much that they won't take the risk. I don't think Raoul has any idea how many people shut down around him.

In fact, most of the people who worked for Raoul were not comfortable talking to him about anything. Some people spent a good deal of their time trying to figure out how not to have to deal with him at all. They would frantically work with others trying to solve a problem rather than have to be the one to go tell Raoul there was a problem. One person summarized the general feeling this way: "I consider myself to have had a pretty good day if I have managed to avoid talking with my boss. Pretty sad, isn't it?"

"When He Walks on the Beach He Leaves No Footprints"

Josh is a manager in a blue-collar work environment. Personally, he is as nice a guy as you could ever hope to meet. He is soft-spoken, kind, and considerate. Employees really like him. Many of them are immigrants to this country, and Josh makes a special effort to reach out to them and help them adjust to working in an American company.

He has a deep commitment to the study of leadership. He attends every class his company offers and others on his own time and at his own expense. He proudly showed me his personal vision statement. It was obvious that he had put a great deal of time and thought into it, resulting in a finely crafted statement of his personal values. In talking about his favorite reading, it immediately became apparent to me that this man, wo had spent some twenty years at work on the shop floor in a manufacturing environment, had actually read more books on leadership than I had. I wound up getting a couple of great reading recommendations from him. I couldn't help but enjoy spending time talking with him, exploring the responsibilities and opportunities of leadership.

Some people might make **great** neighbors, but you **wouldn't want** them to manage people in your **company.**

Unfortunately, my interviews with his direct reports and fellow managers proved to be disappointing. Yes, Josh was a nice guy—no one would argue with that. As long as things were going smoothly, Josh did just fine as a manager. But when it was time for him to actually behave like a leader, he was unable to deliver.

Josh's direct reports complained that they could never count on him to make a decision. Josh was so eager to please everyone that he was unable to act if he felt someone might end up unhappy as a result of a decision he had made. He would constantly defer to a particular direct report who was quite capable and willing to "help" him with his decisions. Over time, she had assumed most of the decision making, acting like an unofficially appointed department head. Josh just found it easier to defer to her than to make decisions on his own.

Josh's direct reports were also unhappy with his failure to back them when there were problems among them. Their role required them to defer to Josh when there were disagreements with the employees. Josh could almost always be counted on to believe the employee's side of the story, leaving supervisors feeling like they were losing all credibility as organizers of their units' work flow. He also failed to "walk the floor," further locking in the impression that there was no management presence where the work was being done.

One of Josh's fellow managers described Josh as "almost invisible" as a member of the leadership team. In her opinion, he was absolutely incapable of making a decision or doing anything at all that required him to take a stand and take any kind of a risk. When I asked what Josh must have been doing with his forty-hour week, she shook her head and said, "I wish I knew." She went on to describe him in terms that struck me as almost poetic, saying that "Josh will turn out to be one of those human beings in life who walked on the beach but left no footprints."

"I'd Rather Do It Myself Than Ask Her to Help"

Julia works in a small branch office of a bank. She is young, working in her first full-time job and going to school at night. She is a member of a small team in a bank office staffed by no more than five or six full-time personnel at any given time. The team works in a confined space, with jobs organized in ways that require a great deal of cooperation and collaboration.

Julia seems to be making an honest effort to contribute as a member of the team. She has mastered most of the tasks required of branch personnel, and she handles money accurately, with few problems balancing her accounts. On the surface, she has the potential to be a good employee. Nevertheless, she is a source of tension on the team, so much so that the bank president felt some external assistance might be helpful.

What I found was that Julia seemed to "have an attitude." She complained about everything. "The break room is too messy." "Management is unreasonable about asking people to come to work early once a week for a team meeting." "The workspace is too crowded." Her list of complaints went on and on.

One bad attitude can create an **unpleasant** work environment for **everyone.**

The bank was in the early phases of transition to self-directed teams. Normally, a manager would have the responsibility of responding to an employee like Julia. But on a self-directed team, it is the responsibility of the team to handle its own problems. Given that the team was in the early stages of learning how to act as its own manager, they were hesitant to raise a difficult issue like this one.

Another factor made Julia even more difficult. She had a way of letting everyone know when she was unhappy about something. For example, if asked to do something she was not inclined to do, she would do what was asked of her but do it in a huff. She would be quiet and sigh frequently. When spoken to, she would respond tersely, using a tone of voice that made it clear to everyone how unhappy she was about being asked to do something she didn't want to do. Yet if people asked her what was going on, she'd respond, "Oh, nothing."

The team was growing tired of Julia's behavior. Working in a small office, it was all the more important for people to be able to get along and create a peaceful work environment. Lately, they had become very reluctant to ask her for help. "Sometimes it's not worth putting up with her suffering," said one person. "I would rather do the work myself than have to ask her for help."

Trusting in Their Good Intentions

This is a book about taking action. But when you work with people like Raoul, Josh, and Julia, it is easy to wonder if there is any point in even trying. After all, how do you work with a "problem person"? How do you make a difference with people who don't seem to care about their impact on the people around them? Is there any reason to hope that a conversation will make a difference?

Your concerns are understandable. Taking action assumes that the other person will respond to your concerns in good faith. Our willingness to approach someone is based on our own assessment of the other person's intentions. It is sometimes easy to conclude that the other person's intentions are anything but honorable.

I have found that sometimes working with a group is a waste of time if certain individuals have not yet come to terms with their impact on the group as a whole. Before moving on to team development with the group, I often find it is necessary to spend some time with individuals who are having a negative impact on the group. Such was the case with Raoul, Josh, and Julia.

These individuals were undermining their teams. They continued to display behavior that was inconsistent with teamwork and collaborative communication. Consequently, my team development work with their groups included individual feedback and coaching before moving on to working with the group. I will discuss Raoul's case as an example.

My meeting with Raoul was like so many of the individual sessions I've experienced over the years. I requested permission to be candid, knowing that he was the kind of person who would want me to be straight with him. I started with something like this:

You have the makings of a great career. You're bright, accomplished, hard working, and highly regarded by your customers. Some of your peers even speak of you as the most obvious choice to succeed the president when he retires in a few years. But what I learned in the interviews leaves me with some serious concerns about your future. Personally, I would hate working for you. People tell me that your leadership style is somewhere to the right of Attila the Hun. Do you want to hear more?

I reviewed my findings in detail, emphasizing his impact on the team and what he needed to do individually if the team development project were going to be successful. He was rather quiet during this meeting. He asked questions to get more details but spent most of the hour listening intently to what I had to say. I gave him a few days to mull over what had been said and to decide what he was willing to do to make the team development project a success.

In our follow-up session a week later, he started by saying something that I have heard so many times before. First, he wanted me to know that he had given a lot a thought to our meeting:

No matter what it might **look like,** most people **mean well.**

I had already scheduled some time off to do some projects around the house. No matter what I was doing, I found myself thinking about our conversation. I was shaken by what my staff said about me. I had long conversations with my wife about it. I also talked with one of my fellow managers, who has known me for a long time. She shared some perceptions of her own that were very much like what my staff had to say. I know that I am demanding to work for, but I had no idea how bad things had gotten.

Raoul had more questions regarding some of my findings, but from the very start of that session he expressed a willingness to act on what I had found.

Raoul's reaction is not all that unusual. Most people want to be successful at work and have a positive influence in the work environment. I don't think I have ever met anyone who gets up in the morning and makes a deliberate decision to drive people crazy at work that day. Can you imagine a business owner getting up and thinking:

What can I do today that will really drive my staff up the wall? How can I sabotage morale and make people so resentful that customer service will suffer? I know! I won't be very clear about what I want from people today. Then, when they ask me questions, I'll look angry and answer the question, but with an expression that suggests they are stupid for not knowing the answer all along. That ought to do it. Boy, is this ever going to be fun!

Can you imagine one of your co-workers going to work thinking:

Things have been going too smoothly around our department. I think I'll go to work today and cause some trouble. I'll make agreements with people and then do whatever I want to do anyway. If people complain about it, I'll act defensive and do my best to make the conversation uncomfortable for everyone involved. That ought to make my day more interesting.

You may work with people who act as if they have consciously made a decision to be hard to get along with. You may have a boss who doesn't like anyone to question a decision he or she has made. You may have co-workers who are always upset about something or who act as if they would rather be doing just about anything other than work with you on some project you've been asked to do together.

Nevertheless, in all the years I've been consulting, I have almost never met anyone whose basic intentions were evil. Most people honestly mean well. Most of them want things to work out well, for both them-

Exercise 10
Walking in the Other Person's Shoes

No matter what it might look like, people who drive you crazy usually have good intentions. Think about someone at work who has been getting on your nerves lately. It may be one of the people you wrote about in exercise 3, "Are You a Victim or a Volunteer?" If more than one person comes to mind, pick the person who is having the greatest impact on your effectiveness or your peace of mind.

- Think about an incident that happened with this person recently.

- Start with an objective description of the situation.

- Now write a description of the incident, but adopt the *other* person's point of view. That is, write the description as if the other person were doing the writing.

- How do you think this person might view the issue?

- What would he or she say about his or her intentions?

- What thoughts, beliefs, attitudes, and needs are leading him or her to behave in a certain way?

- What is he or she trying to accomplish?

selves and their co-workers. It's just that sometimes we all do things that fall short of our good intentions. People who see themselves as one kind of person sometimes behave in ways that are totally inconsistent with their intentions and their professed self-image.

When we have disagreements with people, or when someone is doing something that does not fit our own picture of how things should be, we can't help but see this from one perspective—our own. Then we start reaching all kinds of conclusions about what we think is driving the other person's behavior. Some of these conclusions about others are inaccurate and may damage our ability to see the situation clearly enough to work effectively with the other person. Exercise 10 asks you to try to put yourself in their shoes and see this situation through their eyes.

Taking Responsibility

You have reached a choice point in reading this book. Everything you will read from this point on is about taking responsibility for the way things are for you at work and taking the appropriate actions to make things happen. Doing so, of course, depends on trust.

An Invitation to Trust

When people's behavior is at odds with their good intentions, it is easy to blame them and assume that they are doing these things on purpose and that they don't care about the impact they are having on others. Are you willing to trust that they are doing the best they can to live up to their own values? Can you accept that they might not see themselves as clearly as you might wish? Are you willing to trust that other people are doing what they are doing for reasons that make sense to them?

Lack of trust can be a real stopper of conversations. This is especially true when we take the other person's behavior as the sole indicator of his or her intentions. When we do this, we all too often conclude that those intentions are not honorable, and that a conversation is therefore unlikely to be of any benefit. In fact, it may even be damaging to our career.

Most people mean well, yet their behavior may fall short of their intentions. Provided with the appropriate information so that they can see themselves and their impact on others more clearly, most people are open to a request to make specific changes in how they work with others.

The "Payoffs" of Helplessness

Taking action means taking risks. It means spending time thinking through an issue and how to approach the other person to request a resolution to a problem. Unfortunately, people sometimes get stuck in seeing themselves as a victim of the other person. When this happens, they spend a good deal of time and energy complaining about the other person. They also may be miserable, feeling as though their life at work would be so much better if only the other person weren't such a problem.

I met a manager in a project a number of years ago who turned out to be an object lesson in how much we can wait for changes to occur. He was talking about his boss and what a horrible, untrustworthy person he was thought to be by his staff. "But there is hope," the manager said. "He has a crease in his earlobe."

"He has a *what?*" I asked.

"A crease in his earlobe. I read somewhere that a particular kind of crease in the earlobe is associated with early death from heart attack." He said this with an expression that suggested he was only partly joking. It was almost as if he were waiting for his boss to die so that things would improve for him and the rest of the team!

While this may be an exaggeration, the truth is that I have met many people who are stuck in what looks to them like a hopeless situation that is making them miserable at work. But when I ask if they have done anything about it, the answer is usually no.

Being a victim has its payoffs. If I see myself as the unfortunate victim of an unreasonable boss or an impossible co-worker, then I do not have to take any risks to act and make things different. I may not like what I am getting in this relationship but I also don't have to take responsibility or action. Being a victim leaves the situation entirely out of my hands. I get to be miserable and blame the other person for my misery.

Taking Action Intelligently

Taking action is not about throwing yourself on the point of your own sword. I have seen people who took action, but did so rashly. Sometimes people make a commitment to take a stand with their boss ("I'm not going to take it anymore!"). Then they go to work and say all kinds of things they never should have said. This is definitely, as one of my clients puts it, a "CLA"—a career-limiting activity.

In the pages that follow, we will be looking at strategies for raising even the most difficult issues with others, including the most difficult people. All of this begins with questions we addressed earlier: How am *I* participating in the way things have turned out for me at work? Is there something I have done—or *not* done—that is contributing to the way things are? What can I do now that will make a difference for me, for my co-workers, and for my company? Am I willing to take responsibility and do the work needed to get ready to raise this issue intelligently? Am I also willing to trust that the other person involved probably means well and is doing the best that he or she can do to make things work?

If you are not willing to act, then I suggest you invest your time reading something else. This book will be a waste of your time if you are not willing to apply the information and communication strategies to make something happen. If you are ready to take action, read on.

Chapter Five

When You Are Your Own Worst Enemy

The underlying principle of this book is that almost everyone you work with means well. Now you may be thinking, "If we have such good intentions, why, then, is there so much interpersonal chaos and grief in most of our working histories? If we all mean well, why don't we behave like it? Why do people do things that seem destined to undermine their own success and, sometimes, the success of those around them?"

Saboteurs of Our Good Intentions

There are a number of factors that contribute to our apparent self-sabotage in the workplace. Let's see how many of them may play a role in tripping you up from time to time.

Our Unclear View of Ourselves

One of the saboteurs of our good intentions is that we do not see ourselves very clearly. It is very easy for all of us to see another person's faults and foibles, but when asked to describe our own, that is another matter entirely. If we could see ourselves as others see us, then making some much-needed corrections in our behavior wouldn't be such a problem. Unfortunately, seeing ourselves objectively is not something any of us can do very easily.

It is therefore all too easy to fool ourselves. We may see ourselves very differently from the way those around us see us. For example, we may live happily with the illusion that we are reasonable people who are easy for others to approach. Lacking feedback to the contrary, we can go on for a long time with completely inaccurate perceptions of ourselves.

Each of us is two people: the person we like to think we are and the "evil twin" people have to work with.

Some of these inaccurate perceptions of ourselves can be very damaging to our careers. For example, I might see myself as someone who is very deserving of a particular position or promotion. In reality, however, I may be sorely lacking in the qualities necessary for consideration for such a position. Given that my own sense of myself is so different from that of the people who are making the decision about the promotion, I won't understand why I am not getting the call. I may even end up feeling like those in authority are playing favorites and that I am getting a raw deal. I may assume that others are prejudiced against me because of my race, sex, age, or some other variable. I may then end up feeling wronged and abused when, in fact, my perception of myself is clearly out of alignment with how others see me.

Sometimes we sell ourselves short because of an inability to assess our own strengths accurately. Some people hold themselves back with perceptions of their own unworthiness that do not square with how others see them. I might not attempt, for example, to take a certain training course to qualify for a better job because I don't think I would have a chance anyway. Or I might not put my name in for a particular opening, thinking that I am unqualified, when others might not agree with my own assessment of my potential.

Our Blindness to the Impact We Have on Those Around Us

We can also be blind to ourselves in another way. We can be doing things that have a very strong impact on those around us and not have a clue. This is important to remember as we explore how to raise a sensitive relationship issue with someone at work.

You may work with someone who is doing something that is affecting your ability to do your job well or to enjoy doing it. There are two ways to interpret such a situation. You might assume that the other person is perfectly aware of what he or she is doing and sees how it affects you but does not care. In this case, approaching the person to talk about it probably feels risky and perhaps even pointless. After all, if the other person already knows that what he or she is doing is driving you crazy but doesn't care, how can you expect a conversation to make any difference?

There is another possibility, however. It just might be that the other person is unaware of the seriousness of the impact of his or her behavior on you. You may wonder how this is possible. The truth is that most of us are pretty focused on our own needs and concerns most of the time. It is very easy for us to do things that affect others but not give this much thought. It isn't that we consciously intend to hurt someone's feelings or place an additional burden on a co-worker. We just don't think about it sometimes. Our own needs and responsibilities drive us. We may do things that we would never do if we were to think about it for a moment.

This is especially true when we are under pressure. I might, under most circumstances, be reasonable and polite to my co-workers. But when the heat is on, I might get so focused on what needs to get done that I am more abrupt interpersonally than I normally would be. This might put other people off and leave them thinking that I am a real problem. But remember, I am blind to myself. I don't see that under pressure I am curt and abrupt, cut people off, and all too quickly make decisions without giving much thought to how they will affect others around me. Furthermore, I don't see that when I do this, I alienate people I like as friends and value as co-workers. I may be so focused on getting the job done and meeting a deadline that I end up doing real damage to my relationship with my teammates. And I will have done so without conscious intention on my part.

Let's add more fuel to the fire. Suppose that I am doing things that bother people around me, but that they find this a hard thing to talk about. Lacking information about how I am affecting others, my behavior is unlikely to change. I will continue to do things that negatively affect others but not have a clue that I am doing so. My teammates may think that I know full well how I am affecting them but that I am selfish and don't care. So they won't raise the issue with me because in their estimation, I am the problem, so why bother?

If you are in a leadership position, you may be doing things that severely affect the morale and performance of your team. You may not intend to be having that impact and you may not see it. Nevertheless, there it is and, because you are the boss, your staff will find it difficult to point it out to you. So you will be walking around with one sense of yourself, while your staff may see you very differently and be reluctant to tell you. This sounds like a perfect recipe for a failure of expectations.

The growth in the use of 360-degree feedback devices for use in performance appraisal systems is an outgrowth of this blindness we have for ourselves and its impact on others. In traditional appraisals, only the supervisor or manager provides an assessment of the person's behavior. But if my perception of myself is radically different from how my manager sees me, it is easy to discount his or her perception as biased. When I receive the same feedback from an entire group, I am much more likely to take the feedback seriously.

Our Flawed Personal Logic

Before you dismiss people as complete jerks and judge conversations with them to be pointless, consider the following. People always have a perfectly good explanation for behaving the way they do. It's "perfectly good" in the sense that our account of ourselves always makes good sense to us, no matter how we might be perceived by others.

This is even true of people whose behavior seems to be totally out of step with their stated intentions. Consider Raoul from the previous chapter. In talking to him, several things became clear. First, he really did not see himself clearly at all. He saw himself as challenging where others saw him as unreasonably demanding. He saw himself as setting high standards where others saw him as a perfectionist who was impossible to please. He saw himself as open to disagreement where others saw him as so intimidating that they disagreed with him only when they were absolutely clear about their position. He saw himself as a professional where others found him to be remote and unapproachable.

Second, Raoul did not see the impact he was having on his team. Once he did, it was extremely upsetting to him. He wanted people to be happy and productive in their work. The last thing he wanted was to be so intimidating that people would try to avoid him when he came into their work area. He wanted people to love their work as much as he loved his. Once he began to see the impact he was having on his team, he immediately began looking for ways to make appropriate corrections. In one session I had with him, he made a list of people he felt he needed to approach privately with an apology and a commitment to do a better job as their team leader.

Josh was also oblivious to how he was perceived and his impact on his team, particularly his direct reports. He saw himself as empowering where his fellow managers saw him as abdicating his duty. He saw himself as sensitive to staff needs where his leads saw him as abandoning them. He saw himself as soliciting input and building consensus where his staff found him to be incapable of making a decision.

When I talked to Josh about how others saw him, my feedback was so out of alignment with his own self-concept that he wept openly. For all of his book learning about leadership, he had constructed a view of himself that did not hold up in the light of more objective information. I would love to tell you that Josh saw the light and became a great supervisor. In fact, he ended up choosing a different path. After carefully considering the kinds of personal changes he would need to make to step up to the leadership role, he decided it just wasn't for him. While he understood intellectually that leadership sometimes means making decisions that not everyone will like, he felt it wasn't something he was comfortable doing. In fact, he had always been uncomfortable in the supervisory position. He missed being more involved in doing the work, stating that he felt like he was "at a banquet standing back about six feet from the table, having to watch everyone else eat." He decided to step out of the supervisory role and back onto a line position.

Julia provided another example of our blindness to ourselves. While she knew she had "a tendency to complain a little," she had no idea it was creating a morale problem for the rest of the staff. When I talked to her about her nonverbal communication when asked to do something she didn't want to do, she seemed genuinely puzzled by my feedback. She was also curious why no one had pointed this out to her. I asked her to ask me to do something, just as an experiment. When she did, I sighed loudly, looked petulant, and did what she asked me to do, all the while doing everything I could to let her know how put out I was feeling.

Then I asked her how easy it would be for others to approach someone they work with every day about this kind of behavior. I asked her to remember that they worked in a small office, which made it all the more difficult for people to risk creating an emotional reaction that could taint the atmosphere of the team for some time. Once Julia began to see what she was doing and how difficult it was for others to talk to her about it, she began to see the need for support in making a change. It is taking time, but the team's willingness to point out when Julia falls back into old behaviors is helping. She is not, and probably never will be, a model of perfect graciousness, but at least her team no longer has fantasies about throwing her off the building.

These kinds of behaviors are persistent partly because we do not see ourselves clearly or recognize the impact we have on others. But our behaviors also persist because what we are doing seems to be working. In fact, these behaviors *do* pay off or we wouldn't continue to use them. Consider Raoul. He was successful, had been promoted to a high level at a fairly young age, and was possibly in line to become the next president. Furthermore, when he spoke, his staff moved to respond quickly. On the surface, his behavior seemed to be working.

In order to be motivated to change, he not only had to see the behavior more clearly, he had to see that the costs of behaving this way were ultimately going to outweigh the gains. He was running the risk of losing good people who didn't like working for him. He also had to see that people were so reluctant to give him bad news that no one would tell him about things going on in his department that he needed to know about. Finally, the company was committed to building a more open and participatory environment as a way to improve quality and retain good staff. Given his performance, the president had serious concerns about Raoul's continued tenure in his current position. Performing as he was, there was no way that the president could recommend Raoul to succeed him. Raoul had to see that his behavior was paying off only in the short run. It had worked for him in his career up to now, but the long-term costs were about to become too great for him to pay.

The Strong Pull of Our Personal History

People who communicate very ineffectively at work rarely do so out of a conscious intent to undermine their relationships at work. It is quite to the contrary. They may be trying very hard to make things work, but they are using the only communication tools at their disposal—the tools they brought with them to the workplace.

In order to trust in other people's intentions, it is important to remember where and how we learned to communicate. Every person we see at work brings with him or her a lifetime of experiences that affect how he or she goes about dealing with others. These experiences begin when we are young. From the time we are small children, we start learning how to communicate and get our needs met. And what we learn is powerfully shaped by the circumstances of our early years. On any given team you will find a group of people with incredibly diverse backgrounds and experiences.

In part 2 of this book, a real distinction is made between how one communicates in personal and professional relationships. We are somehow expected to know how to do this, as if it ought to come naturally.

But the people we work with drag behind them years of experience dealing with other people and learning how to get what they want. And where do we learn these coping strategies? We learn them in personal relationships at home, at school, and within peer groups.

Very early in life, we start learning about authority. We learn about conflict and how to cope with it. We learn about what is dangerous to talk about and what should be avoided at all costs. We get many messages about our individual self-worth and what we have a right to expect—or what we have no right to expect at all. We all learn very, very different lessons, depending on our unique circumstances.

Some of us learned that if we are loud, aggressive, and insistent, we will get our way most of the time. Others learned that if they pout and act as if their feelings have been hurt, others will feel guilty and give them what they want. Some learned to be seductive, charming, and ingratiating, saying what others want to hear and manipulating until they get their way. Some, through a series of traumatic experiences at home or with peers, learned that they will *never* get their way, no matter what they do, so there is no point in trying. Still others learned that standing up for what they want is dangerous and that it is best to try to blend into the woodwork, especially when people with authority are anywhere in the vicinity. Then there are those whose life experiences have taught them that life is basically fair and that if they are straightforward, direct, and trusting, things have a tendency to work out for the best.

Think about the amazing diversity of people you knew when you were young. Think about their widely different familial, financial, and educational circumstances. I grew up in a very small town in Iowa, where there was a very homogeneous environment. Yet even here, there was a wide difference in the kinds of kids I grew up with, each of us receiving different messages about our worth and learning different ways to get along in the world.

Now imagine what happens in the workplace. We assemble a group of people with wildly different histories, educational backgrounds, and life experiences. Then we ask them to be "good team players" and tell them

> **We start** learning lessons about ourselves and **about what is possible** for us very early in life. **Then we bring** those lessons **to work with us.**

to go to work. Most of the time, the people on those teams have the very best of intentions—but they lack a common framework for understanding the nature of teamwork and the communication skills necessary to make it work. Sooner or later things begin to break down.

This should not come as a surprise. All of us are a product of our history. There is a great deal of work being done these days on "cultural diversity in the workplace." I have come to believe that we are much more diverse than we think. Diversity runs much deeper than cultural or ethnic backgrounds. In fact, our backgrounds and learned coping skills are so incredibly diverse, I sometimes think it is a wonder that companies function as well as they do. Our ability to get things done, in spite of the diverse perspectives we bring to such loaded issues as authority, conflict, and participation, is a testimony to our commitment and sheer grit.

My own approach to this diversity is to focus first on what it takes to build strong, productive professional relationships. I do that by offering everyone on the team a common perspective on teamwork. What are teams? How do you go about building them? Where do they predictably break down? What is participation? What are the methods for being able to talk about problems with each other without taking things so personally? Start to answer these questions and it is amazing what good-hearted people can do.

Room for Optimism

It is clear that we do not see ourselves clearly, nor do we see how our behavior is affecting other people. We are doing what we do because it makes sense to us—otherwise we wouldn't do it. This simple progression of factors gives me hope. I am called into corporations as a last-ditch effort to save someone whose technical contributions are valued but who has serious difficulties working with people. Time and again, I find people who do not see themselves or the impact they are having on others clearly. Moreover, what they have been doing for so long they are doing because it makes sense to them and seems to be paying off. When given direct and detailed feedback about how others view them, most people want to make the change.

Given that we are blind to ourselves and don't see ourselves the way others do, sometimes we get feedback from others that takes us by surprise. I know this from personal experience. Early in my career, someone told me that I needed to learn to lighten up in front of groups. I was so intent on the message I was delivering that I was coming across as stern and forbidding. This was jarring feedback for me to receive. I didn't see myself as unapproachable. If anything, I was scared to death, trying to build a new business in a big city. I would never have guessed that my physical presentation was undermining my effectiveness in training rooms. I literally had to learn to smile more, tell more jokes, and greet people individually before workshops started in order to break down any barriers I might unwittingly create by concentrating too hard on the message I was trying to deliver.

Sometimes the feedback we receive from others goes to the core of how we see ourselves. A business associate once told me that I was a hard person to disagree with because I didn't listen and let in other points of view. I argued with him that he was wrong, of course. After all, I teach listening skills. Who was he to be telling me I don't use them? He pointed out that I was too busy trying to prove that I was right to really listen to what he was saying. He was right. I wasn't listening. I discovered that this was something I needed to work on. Trying to work through a disagreement with me was sometimes not very much fun. Yet all along, I thought that I was a much better listener than I was in actual practice. The following exercise will help you when you get feedback that takes you by surprise.

Exercise 11
Taken by Surprise

- Think of a time someone gave you feedback that did not fit your self-image, and describe what that person told you.

- In what way was the feedback inconsistent with your view of yourself?

- How did that help you make changes so that your behavior would come into closer alignment with your intentions?

- Now think about the person you wrote about in the previous chapter in exercise 10, "Walking in the Other Person's Shoes." This person may be doing something that has a very negative impact on you. Are you willing to give him or her the benefit of the doubt and trust that, just like you, sometimes his or her behavior fails to live up to his or her good intentions?

As we have discussed, wanting to change, though important, is not enough to ensure that people will be able to actually make the changes. The unseen influence of personal history complicates our best efforts to behave more appropriately. We are shaped by lessons we learned early in life. Some of these lessons came from parents. Others came from teachers and other adults who played significant roles in our lives. The cultural environment we found ourselves in also played a great role in attitudes we developed about ourselves as well as about our self-worth. We also started developing beliefs about other people and ways of communicating to get our needs met.

The following exercise asks you to reflect on some of the early lessons you learned and how some of those lessons may still be influencing you today.

Exercise 12
Reflections on Personal History

- List the adults who were the most influential when you were growing up. In what ways, positive and negative, did they influence how you learned to feel about yourself? In what ways do these feelings about yourself continue to influence you today?

- Adults often talk about work and people at work in the presence of children (who they think aren't paying any attention). As you were growing up, what were some of the beliefs you developed about work as a result of listening to what adults had to say? Think of at least one positive and one negative belief or attitude about work that may still be influencing you today. How have these beliefs influenced choices you have made about work in your adult life?

- Think about where you were raised. In what ways did your early environment limit or expand what you thought would be possible for you in your life as an adult?

- Describe what you learned about communicating in order to get your needs met. For example, I learned early in life that disagreeing with those in authority was frowned upon—rather severely. I also came to see myself as a bit of an oddball around my peers and became very self-conscious and reserved about expressing my feelings and needs. Even today, I sometimes feel like the sixteen-year-old geek who will never fit in. What are some of the early beliefs you developed about yourself, and in what ways do these beliefs limit or expand your ability to make things happen in your life?

- Finally, think about some of your co-workers who may have come from a very different environment. In what ways do you think their current behaviors might be understood, given what you know about their early histories?

The Illusion of Management's "Open Door"

When you are the leader, there are things about you that everyone sees but no one tells you. That is why so many managers get caught up in illusions about themselves. If you are a leader, take a moment to look at things from your employees' perspective. Suppose the person you are having a problem with is your boss. You may have reached the conclusion that your boss is either a jerk or incompetent in some ways that limit his or her effectiveness as a leader. Are you likely to talk about this at all? Not if you have any sense of self-preservation you won't. After all, this is the person who makes choice job assignments, does your performance appraisal, and approves raises and promotions. The last thing you want to do is get on his or her bad side.

This situation creates the conditions for an illusion that is held by many people in management positions. Most managers see themselves as open and approachable, believing that their staff sees them in the same way. You may be newly promoted into a management position. By *management,* I mean any title that puts you in the position to direct the performance of other people. You see yourself as the same person you were before you got the promotion. And, in fact, unless the promotion went to your head, you probably *are* the same person.

But once you are in a leadership position, you have the authority to affect other people's lives. They will never—I repeat, *never*—see you in quite the same way that you see yourself. Many times I have heard managers say, "My door is always open. I am sure that if there was anything bothering people, they would tell me about it." But your staff doesn't see you as the Bob or Mary you were before you got promoted. A difference in power *always* affects relationships and openness. They will always see you as the boss. If they have a problem with you, they are not likely to talk about it. It will seem too dangerous to do so. So you may very well be

Wall's Law: The higher you are in **management hierarchy,** the less you know **what it is like** to work for **you** and **your** company.

A corollary: You think **you know** but **you don't.**

Exercise 13
Shattering the Illusion

- Describe at least two ways in which your actual behavior fails to live up to your own stated values.

- Are you open to properly stated feedback on this aspect of your leadership?

- List actions to take to start living up to your values.

- Take action—today.

walking around thinking things are just fine. At the same time, some of your staff may have genuine concerns about the way things are going in your department. But having reduced the problem to your personality or competence, they will not tell you about it. Lacking the information you need to do a better job leading your team, you continue on your merry way, comfortable with the illusion that if there is something going on, surely they will tell you about it.

Many leaders have a set of stated values and beliefs that they hold to be true about themselves, their leadership, and what they want it to be like to work in their organization. Sometime these stated values stand in marked contrast to how they actually behave.

Leaders are particularly vulnerable to doing things that unwittingly sabotage the effectiveness of the very teams they rely on to make their companies successful. Unfortunately, if you own the company, you have no one there to provide the kind of feedback that would help you see yourself more clearly and make the personal adjustments that would make you more effective. And because you are the boss, you may do things that have a negative impact on your team and no one will tell you. Your team will do the best it can to adjust to your personality and leadership style, all the while wishing things could be different. The following case study provides an example from my own experience.

Case Study of a Company Owner Undermining His Management Team

The owner of a growing company once called me for assistance. When I met with him, he explained that he thought his management team needed training in assertion skills and that they also needed to learn how to manage their teams better. I asked him what led him to believe that a training event was necessary. He complained of a lack of participation in their team meetings:

> *Our management meetings are not very productive. Almost no one participates in the discussion. I call a staff meeting to discuss a problem and they seem reluctant to engage in anything that might produce a useful discussion of issues. I put problems on the agenda for discussion, but they seem reluctant to speak up and help solve the problem. I usually wind up doing most of the talking. It is clear to me that they need assertion training.*

I explained to the owner that he might be right. Training might be an approach that would make a difference. But I went on to share an assumption I make in my consulting—that whatever is going on in a company or a team is somehow a reflection of the person who leads that company or team. If something isn't working, the only useful assumption to make is that the leader is doing something—or *not* doing something—that is contributing to the problem. That is as true for a president leading an entire company as it is for a supervisor leading a team of five within that company. When something isn't working the way you intend, you have to ask yourself what your part of the problem is.

I told the owner that I would be happy to design a course of training events for his company, but that training is sometimes used to fix a problem when some other form of intervention might be more appropriate. I asked if I could do a series of interviews to find out more about the problem. I pointed out that, besides gathering information that would help in the design of a training curriculum, I would be looking closely at the possibility that he was part of the problem. He was skeptical, but he gave me permission to proceed with the interviews.

Conversations with his executive staff quickly supported my hunch that the owner was playing a significant role in how the team meetings were turning out. There were several things he was doing that created a climate that suppressed open conversation. He was an "old school" kind of manager. He had grown up at a time when his particular industry was noted for a top-down, authoritarian approach to management. People were given their orders and expected to do as they were told.

Team meetings were an occasion to be feared. He would review results and harshly criticize anyone whose department was not performing up to his expectations. No matter how good the rest of that team's results might be, he would focus on what wasn't up to par. He would criticize a manager harshly, leading to embarrassing moments when the receiver of the criticism would feel exposed in front of his or her peers. A "good" team meeting was a meeting in which you managed to escape the boss's wrath.

The owner's tendency to focus on the negatives and publicly humiliate people was not exactly conducive to the kind of open discussion of problems that he said he wanted. But there was more. He had a way of suppressing conversation in the team meeting. If someone said something that he didn't agree with, every person in the room would know it. He would get a look on his face that told the person who was speaking at the time that he or she was treading on very thin ice. Continuing to speak might very well get a very abrupt reaction.

He also had some personal habits that shortened conversations. He was one of those high-energy people who have a hard time sitting through meetings, especially if they aren't the one holding the floor. If a discussion actually started to go somewhere and began to take a little time, he would start looking at his watch. He would also drum his fingers on the table, conveying a level of impatience with the discussion that told everyone they had better bring this to a close. Sometimes he would abruptly crumble his coffee cup into a ball, throw it in the trash, and sigh, as if to say, "Are you finished yet?" Is it any wonder the meetings were not very productive?

I felt that training, all by itself, would be a waste of time. I could train his staff, certainly, but would training make any difference in the atmosphere he was creating? I felt that he had to look into his heart and look at how he wanted things to be in his company. It was his company, and he certainly had the right to run it any way he pleased. But if he wanted the creativity and problem solving that comes from open discussion, he was going to have to make some changes. The source of the problem was *the owner himself*, not a skill deficit on the part of his staff.

As we discussed my findings, several things became apparent. First, he was completely oblivious to the impact his behavior was having on the team: "I drum my fingers on the table all the time. It drives my wife crazy. But it's just a habit."

As for the facial expressions, he gave me a golden opportunity to point it out during our conversation. As I was talking about how he was creating an atmosphere in which people feared him, he made a face. "You may not even be aware of it," I said, "but you are scowling at me. If you were my boss and my family's financial security depended on my staying in your good graces, I would be backpedaling right now. That scowl on your face is pretty intimidating."

He looked surprised, for a couple of reasons. First, he is not used to people being that straight with him. But he also went on to explain himself: "I'm not scowling. I am just focusing on what you are saying and trying to understand. I am paying very close attention to you right now."

"If you are interested in what I am saying, you need to communicate that to your face," I told him. "You look like you are angry. Whether you realize it or not, your face seems to be saying that you don't want to hear another word from me."

After more conversation, we decided to call the team together for a meeting. Rather than starting with a formal presentation, he and I had a conversation with each other in the front of the room. This allowed me to ask questions and provided an opportunity for him to talk about himself in a more informal way. He talked about his history in the industry. He told about the "old days," when this had been a "dog-eat-dog" industry in which only the strong survived. He had learned to manage people by observing all the managers he had worked for early in his career. Orders were given. People were held accountable when they didn't get the job done. If you didn't hear anything at all, then you could assume that you were doing a good job. Praise and encouragement were unheard of. Open participation amounted to the words, "Yes, Sir."

He went on to say that he truly wanted to be a better boss than that. Looking back on it, he didn't like the way he had been treated early in his career, and he was dismayed to discover that he was treating his staff the same way. He apologized to the group, saying that he did not want to create an environment in which people hated having to interact with him. He said that he wanted them to know how much he appreciated their hard work and that he wanted their help in building a company that would continue to grow and prosper.

Finally, he talked about his edginess in meetings, about how hard it is for him to sit still sometimes. He asked them to do something that they might find difficult. When he started sending nonverbal messages that they might understand to be impatience, he wanted them to point it out to him. I suggested that they try having a rotating chair for the staff meetings, with each week's chairperson assembling the agenda and leading the discussion of problems that the team needed to address. This would let the team take more ownership of the meeting and allow the president to participate in the discussion rather than be the focal point of every conversation.

Finally, I asked him to reflect for a moment and talk about things his team had done recently that he appreciated but had not commented on. He spoke at length about the hours they had put in and the results they had produced, establishing a strong presence in a highly competitive business environment. He said that when he met with other company owners he always bragged about what a strong management team they were. He asked that an item be added to each meeting's agenda. In addition to problems needing to be discussed, he asked that they also take a few minutes each week to celebrate the company's successes. "We are doing a great job here," he told them, "and we need to talk about what *is* working as well as what isn't. Then maybe we will all be in a better mood to do some problem solving."

A chair for the next week's meeting was appointed, and we discussed a quick method that the group could use to participate in building the agenda before each meeting. The mood in the room could only be described as "tangible relief." People left the room after shaking the owner's hand and telling him how much they had appreciated hearing from him that day and learning more about him. As I was leaving, I suggested we defer assertion training for now, giving him and the team a chance to meet a few times to see how things would work out.

I stayed in touch with him. We never did do that assertion training that he had been so convinced would fix the problem. It wasn't necessary.

Part Two
Fixing the Relationships That Are Not Working

Chapter Six

Diagnosing What Went Wrong

In looking at conflict at work, it is clear what happens when we lack awareness of the inevitable glitches that occur when people work together, and when we don't have a practical framework for understanding how to work together. We end up looking at problems at work as if they were problems with the personality, character, intentions, or capabilities of the other people involved.

In order to change how we deal with our working relationships, we need to change how we think about them. We need to take the concept of *teamwork* to a new level. Instead of some abstract value that everyone agrees is a good thing, we need to bring some simple and practical guidelines for working together into the workplace. These guidelines are necessary if people are to build effective working relationships and identify and resolve the breakdowns in teamwork that always occur, no matter how good a job the group has done in "team building."

A *team* is any group of two or more people who must work together to get something done. You probably participate in a number of teams at work. The most obvious teams are formally defined. You may, for example, be a member of a department or a work group. That group may be part of a larger unit, such as a division. The company as a whole is a team.

On any given day, we flow in and out of any number of teams. Some of these teams are formed quite informally to accomplish work and solve problems. You might be part of a problem-solving group. You might be assigned to work with a co-worker for a couple of hours on a project. You might be working with a customer or a company that supplies goods and services to your company. Any time you work with other people, each

> **Everyone** applauds **"teamwork,"** but we need to **understand how** to make it **happen.**

party involved needs to be clear about how you are going to work together if you hope to get anything done.

Guidelines for Working Together

Few people arrive in the workplace with a practical understanding of what to do to build an effective working relationship. Fortunately, there is a simple set of guidelines to follow. Teamwork on any formally or informally defined team must be built on a foundation of agreements in the following areas:

- *Goals:* What are we going to accomplish?
- *Roles:* What is expected of each member of the team?
- *Procedures:* How will we coordinate our work with each other?

As you will see, these guidelines also provide a way of more accurately diagnosing the source of conflicts that inevitably occur when people work together.

I know from experience that these guidelines for team development work. I was first exposed to goals, roles, and procedures when I participated in an interpersonal skills training project in Iowa about twenty-five years ago. One of the master trainers, Mark Plovnick, shared some research findings from a study done in collaboration with Ronald Fry and Irwin Rubin, his colleagues at the Sloane School of Management at Massachusetts Institute of Technology.

Plovnick, Fry, and Rubin were doing a study of conflict in health care teams. When they asked people about the sources of these conflicts, their answers were usually highly personalized assessments of their co-workers' personalities or capabilities. On closer examination, Plovnick and his colleagues found that these conflicts could best be understood as breakdowns in the team's agreements about how they were going to work together. Lacking a practical understanding of how to build teams and diagnose conflicts, they jumped to the conclusion that they were involved in a personality conflict or that the other people involved were incompetent.

When people work together, they need to reach agreements about goals, roles, and procedures. Then, when conflicts occur, instead of taking things so personally, they need to remind themselves that the problem resides in their professional relationship, one that is based on these mutually understood agreements. Whenever people have a problem working together, paying attention to their goals, roles, and procedures is almost always the surest and safest avenue to a solution.

Once a team produces clarity about teamwork by tuning up their agreements about their goals, roles, and procedures, an interesting thing happens. The team starts functioning at a higher level of effectiveness. When everyone on the team shares the same understanding of the team's goals, roles, and procedures, things get done.

But something else happens as well. Seemingly deep-seated personal issues begin to disappear. It may be that these "personality conflicts" never actually existed. Lacking any other way of understanding teams and conflict, the team members jumped to conclusions about each other when teamwork began to break down. Once we start focusing on our working relationship and reach greater clarity about goals, roles, and procedures, our personal issues with other people begin to resolve themselves.

Why Teams Break Down

I use the language of goals, roles, and procedures as a way of assessing teamwork in my consulting projects. When I do a study of an organization, I have limited time and a limited number of interviews with team members to make an assessment of a situation. In my interviews, I listen for at least two things. First, where have relationships broken down due to personalized conflicts that have left team members feeling estranged from each other? Second, how can these conflicts be resolved be reaching agreements about the team's goals, roles, and procedures? After all these years, I have yet to find a more useful way of sorting out relationship problems at work. This method works.

In assessing your own teamwork at work, it is helpful to remember that agreements regarding goals, roles, and procedures are subject to the following kinds of problems: ambiguity, incompatibility, overload, and disagreement.

Ambiguity

The most common source of problems in teamwork is ambiguity. Team members may be very busy and may not take the time to ensure that everyone on the team shares the same understanding of their agreements regarding goals, roles, and procedures. Sometimes leaders assign a task to a team, taking it for granted that the team will be able to work effectively together.

When we assume that everyone sees teamwork in the same way, we leave the team open to conflicts that are then taken personally. I have seen the following sequence played out time and again:

- The team's goals, roles, and procedures are not clearly defined.
- Individual team members begin making their own assumptions about goals, roles, and procedures.
- These assumptions may differ from conclusions reached by other members of the team.
- People start pursuing differing goals with the added confusion of misunderstandings about each other's roles and the procedural agreements necessary to coordinate the group's work.
- When teamwork breaks down, people react emotionally in the heat of the moment, assuming that their own understanding of the group's goals, roles, and procedures is correct and that this should be obvious to the rest of the team.
- As the problems persist, individuals begin to reach the conclusion that others in the group are either "jerks" or "incompetents" or both.
- Given this diagnosis, people may lash out at each other emotionally or attempt to work on in frustrated silence.
- Over time, trust within the team suffers significant damage, making the repair of working relationships all the more essential and, at the same time, all the more difficult.

Ambiguity about teamwork **is a fast track** to conflict **that gets taken** personally.

Incompatibility

Some of the team's goals, roles, and procedures may be incompatible or inconsistent with other goals, roles, and procedures. For example, a team may have one set of goals targeting world-class customer service and another for reducing the cost of labor and materials. These conflicting goals will sooner or later leave the team in the bind of trying to provide great service without the resources needed to make it happen.

Overload

Sometimes goals and roles are clearly defined but leave people overloaded. Overload plays out in the following way:

- Highly motivated people take on too much, agreeing to extreme goals or roles that include excessive expectations.
- Committed to keeping their agreements, people work longer and longer hours, a strategy that appears to work for a time.
- Unless management pays close attention to the quality of life in the organization, long hours become the standard expectation rather than a heroic response to a temporary crisis.
- Individuals begin to suffer from predictable negative impact on their personal relationships outside of work as well as on their physical health and energy.
- In time, some people begin to look for positions in other companies, in hopes of creating a better balance of work and play in their lives. Others may stay with the company but suffer from burnout and lack of enjoyment in the work itself.
- Teams show signs of a tired, frustrated staff. Short fuses result in damaged relationships as otherwise responsible people cope poorly with conflict.

Disagreement

Teamwork breaks down when members of the team either do not reach or do not honor agreements about their goals, roles, and procedures. For example, a team can have problems because of continued and unresolved disagreement among some of its members about priorities. Time can be lost to the replay over and over again of the same discussions between parties who have not reached resolution about what is to be done and how they will work together to accomplish it.

Ask too much from too few for **too long** and even the most **stable teams** will show the **strain.**

Disagreement about teamwork can also result in covert resistance to resolving the uncertainty. For example, a team member may have a fixed idea about what role she wants to play on the team. However, she may fear that a discussion of this matter will result in an answer she doesn't want to hear. She prefers to let the question linger unexamined, giving her the latitude to continue to do what she wants to do anyway, all the while trying not to draw the kind of attention that will result in a more open resolution of the matter. After a while, this kind of subtle sabotage of the team's developmental process results in resentment from the rest of the team that affects overall morale.

Identifying Goals

One might think that the need for agreement about goals would be obvious. If people are going to work together, they had better reach a mutually understood agreement about what they are to accomplish. Yet look at your own experience. I am willing to bet you have experienced frustration at work because you thought your team was supposed to accomplish one thing, yet someone else appeared to be going off in a different direction.

Unless you are more disciplined than most people I know, you have probably personalized this conflict from time to time. Whenever teamwork breaks down, we have the opportunity to jump to conclusions about the personality or competence of someone else. Imagine yourself working under a tight deadline. You think you know what the team is supposed to accomplish. In the middle of all your hard work, you notice that one of your teammates is going off in what is, to you, the wrong direction. Like most of us under pressure, you may not be thinking as clearly as you might under other circumstances. You may begin to have thoughts such as these:

As **Yogi Berra** once said: "**The problem** with unclear goals **is that** you just **might** achieve them."

What in the world is Helen doing? She knows what we are supposed to get done by the end of the day. There she is, working on something we aren't supposed to do until tomorrow. That is just like her. What a space cadet! She couldn't understand directions if you wrote them in large block letters and read them to her. All she cares about is what she wants to do.

The problem with this kind of thinking is that it short-circuits our ability to talk about the problem productively. Start a conversation by calling someone a "space cadet" and see how far it goes. If Helen is your boss, you probably won't talk about it at all but will continue to work in disgruntled silence. As so often happens when we start focusing on the other person as the deliberate or bumbling cause of a problem, it doesn't occur to us that the other person actually means well and that maybe there is some confusion about our teamwork. It won't occur to us to have a conversation that starts something like this: "Helen, we need to talk. I thought we were supposed to do one thing. Apparently you think we're supposed to do something else. Can we talk for a moment and clarify our goals to make sure that we are all pushing on the same wall of the box?"

Note that there is nothing personal going on here—we just have a tendency to experience it that way. If people are going to work together, they need to share the same understanding about what they are to accomplish. Sometimes all that is needed for things to start moving in the right direction is for one person to step forward and start a conversation about the right thing—in this case, goals.

Defining Roles and Expectations

For people on a team to work effectively, each person must understand what is expected of him or her and what other members of the team will be doing to ensure that the team achieves its goals. Clearly defined roles are important to both individuals and groups within the team. For example, the role of a given team is open to misinterpretation by other teams. This can lead to conflict between groups. Suppose, for instance, you have three different shifts working in the same area. The team for each shift needs to know what is expected of it, and the other shifts involved need to share the same understanding. In consulting projects, I often hear complaints about the night shift failing to do something the day shift felt they should be doing. This then gets personalized, with people on days thinking that the people on nights are lazy and irresponsible. The night shift, in turn, may feel that the day shift is being overly demanding and expecting too much of them. Note that these assessments of each other—lazy, demanding—have nothing to do with what is really going on. The night shift simply has a different understanding of its role. All that is needed is a conversation to clarify mutual expectations. All this emotionalizing about each other turns out, in the end, to be a mental detour we'd have been better off without.

Disagreement about roles is a frequent source of intensely emotional and disruptive conflict. Suppose someone is doing something that you feel is your job to do. In the heat of the moment, it is easy for you to take this personally and for the conversation to spiral out of control. There you are, working hard and scrambling to keep up. Then Elmer comes into your area and starts doing something that is clearly (to you, anyway) on your to-do list. You are certain that this is a role your boss assigned to you.

It is all too easy for you to jump to the conclusion that Elmer doesn't care about agreements, doesn't honor your role, and hasn't given a thought to how you might feel about him taking over a task you thought was yours to do. You may even see this as evidence that Elmer doesn't trust you to do your job and that he thinks he'd better do it himself. You now have the ingredients you need for an emotional outburst. In the middle of all your assessments about Elmer, it may not occur to you to remind yourself that there really is nothing personal going on here. Apparently Elmer has one understanding of what each of you is to do, while you seem to have a different understanding. The situation isn't all that complicated. In fact, it is only a conversation away from resolution. But in the middle of all the personalizing, conversations sometimes go awry—or they don't happen at all.

Establishing Interpersonal Procedures

There are two kinds of procedures that enable teams to function: technical and interpersonal. In a health care environment, for example, there are all kinds of technical procedures to ensure that care gets delivered in a consistent way across three shifts a day, day in and day out. These procedures need to be clearly described, and people must be trained to follow them.

For instance, the distribution of medications is a critically important aspect of care in a hospital. Imagine the danger to patients if nursing staff across three shifts developed their own procedures for dispensing and documenting medications. Without standardized procedures, one shift would very soon lose track of what other shifts had or hadn't done. This would result in patients either getting too much of what they need or not getting anything at all. Procedures, clearly defined and followed, ensure that everyone dealing with patients takes a consistent approach to this important task.

Other procedures are softer, more interpersonal in nature. For teams to work together, we need to have procedures that tell us how information is shared. We need to have agreements about how resources are deployed so that every member of a team knows what is available and how to tap into the supply when it is needed. These interpersonal procedures represent a complex web of communicating and coordinating functions that enable a team to work as a unit.

Both technical and interpersonal procedures are subject to one source of confusion. Procedures are often defined in two ways, formally and informally. The formal definition of procedures may be presented in nicely documented and bound manuals and may be the subject of staff training events. But there may also be a more informal and unwritten set of procedures that may be in direct conflict with the formal procedures. It's as if there is the official way we do things and then there is the way we *really* do things. This can sometimes be confusing, especially to new staff who are trying to figure out how things get done. It can also lead to conflict when some people try to do things "by the book," serving as a source of real irritation to those who prefer the more informal way of getting things done.

> **If** doing things **"by the book"** is quite **different** from how things **get done** in actual practice, it might be **time to rewrite** "the book."

Professionalizing Conflicts

In truth, personality conflicts do occur. It is just that they occur far less often than we think they do. Most conflicts at work are the result of a breakdown in our professional relationships. Some ambiguity or disagreement about goals, roles, and procedures is making it difficult for us to work together. In the heat of the moment we have personalized the conflict, attributing it to the personality or incompetence of the other person.

Professionalizing conflict offers an alternative to the risks and emotions of personalized conflict. When we *personalize* an issue, we assume that the source of the problem resides in the personality or competence of the other person. We also end up focusing on feelings of hurt, anger, resentment, and fear. If we talk about the issue at all, our feelings and assessments of the other person often end up derailing the conversation.

To *professionalize* a conflict is to remind ourselves that the most likely cause of the problem isn't personal at all. The problem can best be understood as a breakdown in our teamwork. Both parties mean well and probably have the skills they need to do the job well. It's just that we have some misunderstanding that is interfering with our ability to work together effectively. We need to stop making assessments of each other's personalities and capabilities and start talking about how we are going to work together.

If we can remember to pause for a moment and remind ourselves not to take things so personally, we are on the way to finding a solution to the problem. Remember this: if the issue is interfering with your ability to work collaboratively with another person or team, the resolution almost always lies in some conversation about your mutual understanding of your team's goals, roles, and procedures.

If you are like most people, you have recently experienced a conflict at work that ended up feeling like a clash of personalities. The following exercise will help you with the first step in resolving conflict, which is professionalizing the issue, using the language of goals, roles, and procedures to more accurately diagnose the source of the problem.

Teams and Relationships on the Brink

Building a successful company poses challenges to relationships that are inevitable and often unanticipated. The most difficult challenge some companies face is growth. As they add new people and develop new parts of the organization, companies run the risk of losing the special quality that made them successful in the first place, as the following case study shows.

Exercise 14
Taking Conflict out of the Personal Realm

- Pick a conflict that is currently of concern to you.

- Describe the situation. Be sure to include your feelings about the other person and any assessments you may have about the other person's intentions, character, or personality.

- Now see if you can describe the issue as involving some ambiguity or disagreement that is affecting your professional relationship. Are your goals unclear, taking the two of you in different directions? Are your roles ambiguous, leaving the two of you at odds over who is supposed to do what? Are procedural problems contributing to the problems between you?

- How have personalized assessments of each other disrupted your ability to resolve problems in your working relationships?

Case Study of the Relationship Challenges Posed by Success and Growth

I once worked with a company that was experiencing some relationship problems that were quite puzzling to the company's owner and president. "We ought to be feeling great right now," he said.

We are succeeding even beyond the rather ambitious plans we put in place a couple of years ago. Our market share is expanding, sales are up and climbing, and the coming year looks even better than the one we are just completing. But there is a level of tension and conflict on my management team that I just don't understand. Some of these people have worked together for years. We have never had these kinds of problems in the past. Some of them I consider to be my friends after all this time, but everything seems so strained lately. I am also hearing about problems out in the rest of the organization that concern me. What is going on here?

I have seen this before in companies that started small and then began to expand to meet the needs of a growing customer base. Consider what happened in the early stages of building one company. The owner of this company runs a chain of retail and service stores. In its early years, the company was quite small. The entire management team could sit around the table at the same time. Given the challenges of starting and running a new company, the team was driven by the spirit of "one for all and all for one." There was a great deal of work to do and not many people to do it. Roles were loosely defined, with people volunteering to take on projects and do whatever was needed, all in the interest of building a successful business.

The original management team spent many hours together in their early years in business. Close friendships developed as everyone worked together, with many feeling that the owner was not only their boss but at times almost an older brother or a close friend. They had developed a way of working together that was truly special, with team members feeling a quality of love and friendship that made the work they did more enjoyable and the long hours less of a burden.

Had the organization stayed the same size, the relationships would have remained close and collegial. The response from the marketplace, however, dictated growth. New locations were added. More managers needed to be brought into the inner circle. As the new locations were being developed, the owner got so busy that he was no longer as available to the group as he had been. He couldn't be. He had too much work to do.

The relationships within the group began to show the strain of change. People who were used to the luxury of having long conversations with the owner rarely saw him. When they did, the conversations were briefer and more focused on immediate business issues. The personal comfort and closeness that used to be so special began to slip away.

Then the owner did something that was organizationally necessary but very difficult for people who had been there from the early days to accept. He realized that the management team was getting so big that he could no longer manage the details of the business himself and continue to serve as the visionary entrepreneur, creating new locations and expanding the company's services. He needed to bring someone in to manage the company, freeing him up to do what he did best—build a great company.

The original members of the management team had a difficult time adjusting to the impact of the success they had helped create. The changes hit them at two levels, personal and professional. There once had been an inner circle that was involved in almost all facets of running the company. As the organization expanded, however, efficiency demanded that the team members' roles be much more clearly defined. It was also necessary to begin to ask who needed to be involved in specific decisions, meaning that some people would no longer be at every management meeting unless the topic required their input.

While the managers understood intellectually the need to use their time more efficiently, it left them feeling less involved than they used to be. They also felt less important. But the most difficult change for them to accept was the change in their personal relationship with the owner. He was so distracted by opening new outlets that they were not getting the quality time with him that they used to find so satisfying. They began to feel a personal distance from him that some took as evidence that they were not as important to him as they had been.

Then there were all the new people to get used to. The original team resented them in ways that they were embarrassed to admit. New people came in with new ideas and new ways of doing things. Sometimes the original staff felt that their own histories and accomplishments were being discounted by these interlopers who were "coming in and changing things without a clue what it took for us to get to where we are today."

The new staff, on the other hand, were confused. They couldn't understand what all the fuss was about. All they knew was that they had been asked to join and contribute to an exciting and successful enterprise. They encountered a resistance to change and a level of personal discontent that they did not understand or know how to cope with. Over the course of a couple of years, the group established a new equilibrium, and the company is still doing quite well.

Here are some conclusions I've drawn over the years of working with companies coping with the challenges posed by success:

- *It isn't the same company anymore.* If your company is growing, it can't be the same company and continue to succeed. New people will be added at all levels. Roles will shift and become more specialized. There will be a lot of new people to get to know and develop a working relationship with. The "old-timers" won't feel as involved in everything as they used to. This is often a difficult adjustment for people, but it is inevitable as companies grow.

- *Leaders must pay special attention to relationship maintenance.* If people begin to see far less of a leader they have come to consider a friend as well as their boss, it is easy for them to conclude that they are not as valued as they used to be. In spite of the busyness that comes with growth, leaders need to take the time to assure their long-term associates that they are valued and important. Otherwise, some people will become so unhappy that they will begin to wonder if they shouldn't be looking for a new place to work.

  The irony is that sometimes leaders will spend less time with certain individuals because they trust them so much that they feel they can put their attention on more pressing concerns. Unfortunately, spending less time with an important relationship is easy to misinterpret. Being trusted to function with less attention and one-on-one time can easily be experienced as a loss of a personal relationship.

- *The organization's needs may outstrip the abilities of long-term staff.* As organizations grow, their needs expand. Sadly, this sometimes means that someone who may have functioned in a particular role for years no longer has the ability to keep up with the growing needs of the organization. For example, someone may have done a fine job with the financial and accounting side of the company when it was smaller. But as the organization grows, the leader comes to the realization that the company needs someone with a broader background and a deeper set of skills. This may result in needing to demote or replace someone who helped make the company successful. If the company now needs a chief financial officer, some difficult personnel decisions may have to be made. This not only affects the person who currently has that role in the company, but it also affects the other members of the team who are already grappling with the impact of growth and change.

- *Sometimes newer staff run into resistance and even resentment. If* you are one of the newer staff in a growing company, be patient. You have to understand that the people who helped build the company in its early days may be having a difficult time adjusting to the professional and personal changes that come with building the organization and adding all these new people in new roles. Don't take the resistance personally. Remind yourself that you would probably be having some of the same feelings if you were in their shoes and that, in time, most people will adjust to the new state of the organization.

Every team, without exception, is subject to breakdowns in teamwork. The following exercise will help you identify problems in teamwork within your department and professionalize your team's internal teamwork.

Dealing with the Toughest Relationships

Now you may be thinking about someone at work who has really been giving you fits lately. Perhaps it's your boss. Maybe it's a co-worker. You may be thinking, "Yes, I can see how this situation involving Fred could be seen as resulting in ambiguity about our roles. I suppose a conversation to achieve greater clarity in roles would enable us to work together a little better. At the same time, in my heart of hearts, I still think Fred is a jerk!"

Genuine personality conflicts do in fact occur. Sometimes we have to work with people who seem to be genetically predisposed to jerkness. And we all have days when we fail to live up to our own standards for ourselves. We may have had an upset at home before coming to work in the morning. We may be thinking about some financial crunch that con-

Exercise 15
Assessing Your Team's Teamwork

- List examples of goal ambiguity or disagreement that impede your team's ability to work effectively.

- List examples of role ambiguity or disagreement that impede your team's ability to work effectively.

- List any procedural problems affecting your team.

- Review the list. Identify those breakdowns in teamwork that have gotten so personalized that emotions are making it difficult for those involved to see the issues clearly and talk about them effectively.

- Identify problems in teamwork affecting your team's ability to work with other teams.

- Identify situations when other teams may have different understandings of your mutual goals, roles, and procedures.

- Identify the team involved and the person you might want to approach for a conversation to resolve the problem.

- Don't do anything yet. First study the chapters on raising issues. You will then be better prepared to act professionally and persuasively.

cerns us. Or we may be tired and frustrated from working too many hours on a difficult project. As a result, we are having a bad day. We don't listen to people as intently as we normally would. We aren't as open to disagreement. We aren't as tolerant of frustration or problems as we might like to be. If you have such days yourself, you just have to know that at times your co-workers are subject to these same kinds of pressures. We need to give each other some room to be human once in a while and not take things so seriously.

But even when the person you have to work with really is a certifiable jerk, you still have to make a choice. If someone's behavior is interfering with your teamwork, then your conversation can go one of two directions. You can take the low road and lash out. You may even find some satisfaction in telling this person what a pain he or she is. We often justify these personal attacks under the guise of "being honest" and "taking care of myself by asserting my own needs." Unfortunately, personal attacks rarely end well at work. At the very least, you end up with a co-worker with whom it is even more difficult to get along.

The guidelines for working together of goals, roles, and procedures offer you a safer, less emotional, and more productive entry into the conversation. Rather than talking about someone's character and apparent disregard for the needs of other human beings, you can instead focus on how to work more effectively together and sidestep the issue of personality and character altogether. I would much rather approach someone about a need to clarify our roles than talk about his or her "obvious" lack of sensitivity to what other people are trying to accomplish as members of this team. This requires careful preparation and a disciplined approach to delicate conversations, a topic we will get to when we start looking at communication strategies.

When **people** stop **worrying** so much about **their feelings** and focus on **teamwork,** even the toughest working relationships **can improve.**

No one ever said that you have to like everyone you work with. If you work on a large team, there may well be someone on your team who makes your skin crawl. The two of you seem destined not to get along. This happens for a lot of reasons. You may not like the other person's personality. Your values may differ radically on some very important issues.

Unfortunately, when two people do not get along personally, this may lead to breakdowns in their professional relationship. Teamwork takes constant attention and conversation to resolve emerging problems stemming from changes in our goals, roles, and procedures. If we do not like someone, we may avoid talking to him or her, even when we need to. This leads to problems in both of our relationships with this person—professional and personal. The following exercise will help you get ready to work more effectively with a certifiable jerk.

Exercise 16
Working with a Certifiable Jerk

- Is there someone on your team you personally dislike?

- If so, review your professional relationship. Are there any conversations you need to have with the person regarding your mutual understandings of your goals, roles, and procedures?

- If so, read chapters 8 and 9 to prepare you for these conversations.

Chapter Seven

Participating in Decision Making

If there is any one theme that captures organizational development in the nineties, it is the effort to get employees and teams more involved in making decisions about issues that affect their work. So much work has been done in the last ten years or so that you can read entire books on continuous quality improvement, self-directed work teams, participatory management, and a host of related topics. I have no intention of offering a comprehensive review of the participatory movement in this book. Rather, I want to share my understanding of the need for participation and how to better define and expand your participation in decisions that affect your job.

A New Way of Thinking About Problems in Organizations

W. Edwards Deming was the source of a movement focused on continuous quality improvement through expanded employee participation. He devoted his life to helping companies produce higher-quality goods and services while realizing astounding cost savings through the reduction of waste, errors, and inefficiency.

Deming's contribution, I believe, centers on an observation about how we think about problems in organizations. In the traditional way of thinking about how things should be done, there is a right way and a wrong way to do any given job. Management's role is to first make sure that people are told how to do their job properly and then make sure they do it. For a long time, we believed that if we could just establish enough control over people so that everyone did his or her job properly, as defined by management, then your business would be successful.

This led to an obvious response by management to problems on the job. It was management's job to tell people what to do and the employees' job to do it. If there were a problem, then there must be an individual to blame. After all, if everyone would just do his or her job properly, then there wouldn't be any problems, right?

This way of thinking led to the development of a fairly heavy-handed approach to management. Look back on management texts prior to the last ten to fifteen years and you will see that, among other things, a manager's job was to organize, direct, and control. You will also find a heavy emphasis on discipline and strategies to make sure people performed as directed. Errors, it was thought, must be the fault of the worker. Therefore, errors required a corrective response by management—with the proverbial whip, if necessary.

An observation by Deming led to a revolution in both how we structure organizations and how we see the role of leaders and of the people on the line who build products and deliver services. Deming was interested in discovering the source of errors, waste, and inefficiency. Every error, every incidence of waste, every example of inefficiency could be attributed to one of two causes:

- *The individual worker.* Sometimes errors, waste, and inefficiency are due to the individual worker. The person isn't trained properly. He or she doesn't care about the job and does things poorly. Someone is having a bad day and not performing up to expectations. A person has problems with addiction and comes to work incapable of getting anything done. For these and many other reasons, problems in getting things done can be traced back to an individual worker who is responsible.

- *The system.* Sometimes errors are not the fault of the individual worker. The problem is caused by the system within which individual workers and teams do their jobs. This system is much larger than any one individual and is beyond any one person's capacity to control. Problems in the system can take many forms—for example, how work is organized, how we communicate, how we use resources, and a host of other factors that determine how effectively individuals and groups are able to get their work done. When there are problems in the system, the individual worker may be working very hard, but the system itself is generating errors, waste, and inefficiency.

Deming posed an interesting question. Suppose you take all of an organization's errors, waste, and inefficiency and put them in one of two piles. In one pile, put all the problems that are the fault of individual workers. In the other pile, put all the problems that are caused by the system within which individuals do their work. What percentage of problems will wind up in each pile?

Deming asserted that only 15 percent of problems could be attributed to any given individual worker. The remaining 85 percent of errors, waste, and inefficiency are due to problems in the system. I am told that toward the end of his life, Deming had changed his opinion about the 85/15 ratio. He had come to believe that the actual ratio might be closer to 95 percent systems problems, with only 5 percent (or less) due to the individual worker

Consider what this means. Let us suppose for a moment that managers in a certain company were able to control individual performance perfectly, thereby ensuring that every single person would do his or her job exactly as he or she was told. Even if this level of control were possible, we would have managed to eliminate only 5 to 10 percent of the errors, waste, and inefficiency present in the day-to-day operations of their company. Most problems are bigger than any one person. The source of most of our problems can be found in the systems that have so much impact on the people who are trying to do their jobs properly.

I am using the term *systems problem* broadly. You have a job to do as an individual. You are probably a member of a team composed of people who are doing similar work. This team needs to coordinate its work with other teams that make up the company as a whole. By *system* I am referring to the complex array of communications tools, documentation procedures, procedural requirements, and endless other methods and processes used to orchestrate the work of the group as a whole. Any one aspect of the system may make sense to the person who designed it but end up creating problems, waste, errors, and inefficiency for other people and teams elsewhere in the company. These problems may then be misinterpreted as revealing the need to train or discipline workers so that they will finally get things done right, as the following case studies show.

Suppose you want to identify problems in the system that are affecting performance. Who is in the best position to know about them? The answer is frontline workers, of course. They are the people who are

Case Studies of Misunderstood Systems Problems

There's an Attitude Problem

A factory foreman felt disciplinary action was needed to correct the performance of workers who continually made errors in loading trucks with orders to be delivered to customers. He felt they had an "attitude problem," that "young people today just can't be counted on to do an honest day's work." Further examination revealed that the way in which customer orders were relayed to the floor was unwieldy and difficult to use in a fast-paced environment. The team faced a heavy demand for the quick loading and dispatching of trucks. They were doing their best to fill the orders properly and quickly, but the paperwork was cumbersome and difficult to read, making it almost impossible to complete the orders in a hurry without making errors. Simplification of the order procedures and documentation reduced errors and speeded up the process. Clearly, discipline was inappropriate.

A corporate trainer was asked to provide training for a team to correct errors that their manager attributed to a skill deficit. He thought more training would surely solve the problem. On closer examination, the trainer discovered that people were in fact making errors implementing changes in an inventory tracking system. But the problem turned out to have nothing to do with the need for training. A project team had been formed to make changes in the tracking system. They were actually doing a good job of improving the system, but they were failing to fully inform the rest of the people affected by those changes, particularly those on the evening shift. A simple "change log" for people to review when coming in for their shift solved the problem. No training was necessary.

Deviating from "The Book"

A foreman at a shipyard was concerned about the high cost of replacement components for electronic equipment. He felt that the vendor supplying the original parts was providing substandard equipment and that the company should go to the expense of calling for new bids to find a new supplier.

Closer examination found that the yard's maintenance requirements were creating the problem. The equipment involved was delicate and needed frequent calibration. Whenever a part needed attention, the maintenance procedures required that the entire unit be removed and sent to the shop for cleaning, testing, and calibration. This could take up to two days, delaying the release of the vessel for use, all for the sake of a minor repair of a component costing less than a thousand dollars. Over time, crews had developed one of those informal procedures that differ so radically from how "the book" said they were supposed to get things done. Whenever a unit needed to be pulled and sent to the shop for repair, they would mark the component as damaged beyond repair and replace it with a brand-new unit. This informal practice had been in place for so long that no one could remember when it had started. A change in the maintenance policy made it possible for the crew to repair and calibrate the unit on site, a process that took less than an hour. In reviewing the problem, the foreman estimated that the company had probably spent well over $100,000 over the last five years replacing entire electronic units that could now be repaired and calibrated on site for a fraction of the cost of a new unit.

closest to the system. They are in the best position to see how limitations in the system are having an impact on how effectively they are able to get things done. Management cannot see the system as clearly as the people who work for them. They aren't close enough to the operations of the system to understand what works and what doesn't work and what needs to be improved.

So the workers are the most likely to have knowledge about the workings of the system. But who, in the traditional way of structuring organizations, has the authority to make changes in that system? The answer is management, of course.

There you have the reason for so much work being done to open up participation on the job. The people who do the work have the knowledge of problems in the system, but they have lacked the authority to change it. Managers have the authority to make changes in the system, but they don't have a clue about what is really going on within the system they are supposed to be overseeing. They need to start talking to each other.

Clarifying Roles for Participation in Decision Making

The participatory movement of recent years has been working on breaking down the barriers between management and the people who do the work necessary to build products and deliver services. While there are a variety of structures being developed to encourage participation, ranging from quality circles to self-directed teams, what these models of organization all have in common is the invitation for teams to participate in how decisions get made. This is certainly a praiseworthy intention. Nevertheless, participation in decision making is tailor-made for creating misunderstandings within teams and between management and staff. What we need is a way of better understanding everyone's role in the decision-making process.

Fortunately, there is a very simple way of sorting this all out. Let's return to the guidelines for working relationships we discussed in the last chapter and expand our definition of roles with respect to participation in decision making.

If you or your team is affected by any decision, you must play one of the following three roles in the decision-making process:

- Decision maker
- Person consulted before the decision is made
- Person informed after the decision is made

In this section, we will take a closer look at each of these roles, particularly that of decision maker.

Who Has the "D"?

One of the most important questions to ask on any team is who has the authority and responsibility to make any particular decision—commonly referred to as the "D." On any given team, it could be argued that there is only one person who has the D. That person is the person at the top, the "Big D."

A few years ago, I led a retreat for the vice president of a bank. Before the retreat, she purchased a "letter sweater," one of those sweaters fans of college teams wear to games. The sweater she bought sported a large "D." It was her joking reference to just who had the D on her team. But imagine the problems she would create if she actually meant it. Suppose she were to try to retain the D on every single decision necessary for her team to function. What would happen? Nothing. Everyone would be standing in a long line outside her office, waiting for her to make the myriad decisions necessary for her division to function on a daily basis. So the D, of necessity, has to flow out from her office to the rest of the team in order for people to make decisions and get things done.

When I think of a hierarchical form of organization, I think of a hierarchy of D's. The president cannot make every decision necessary for a company to do its business. So D's are delegated down to the next level. Executives can't make all the decisions within their area of responsibility, so D's are passed down to managers, who in turn pass D's down to supervisors, who in turn pass D's down to staff. The allocation of decision-making authority is one of the most frequent sources of breakdowns in teamwork.

Conflict on teams can arise from lack of clarity or agreement about who has the decision-making authority or from failure of the person who has such authority to exercise it.

Ambiguity About Who Has It

It may be unclear who has the authority to make any particular decision. Sometimes this leads to inaction. People may arrive at different conclusions about who has the D and delay action, waiting for a decision to be made by the person they think should make it. In other cases, two people or groups may each decide that *they* have the D, resulting in conflict when each attempts to use decision-making authority that they thought was theirs alone.

Sometimes all it takes to resolve the ambiguity about who has the decision-making authority is for one person to simply ask who has the authority. That one question is often the catalyst for a conversation that may resolve a long-standing problem in teamwork. The question focuses the group's attention on one of the most frequent sources of breakdown on teams: lack of clarity about where decision-making authority may reside regarding a specific decision. I sometimes get the chance to return to a company I might have worked with as much as ten years earlier. *Who has the D?* is a concept I often find has stuck like glue since the last time I worked with the company. I think this is testimony to how frequently breakdowns in teamwork begin with ambiguity about exactly where the decision-making authority resides.

Disagreement About Who Has It

Sometimes the source of conflict is very clear—two or more individuals or teams may be in frank disagreement about who has the authority over a particular decision. The only way around this issue is through it. The people involved must be able to discuss this issue and arrive at an agreement about who has the D. It is the only way things can work.

Unfortunately, the issue of authority is one that is easily personalized. Suppose you think you have been given the D regarding the use of certain resources. One day, you come into your area to discover someone making decisions you thought were yours to make. In the heat of the moment, it is easy to jump to the conclusion that the other person involved is intentionally disregarding your role. When you are caught up in emotions, it is hard to remember that the other person probably means well. He or she just has a different understanding about who has the D in this particular situation. The two of you need to talk. The solution is just a conversation away.

Sometimes the D resides with more than one person. The sharing of the D is sometimes necessary, but it creates the opportunity for confusion and conflict. Joint decision making can be made to work, but it is obviously more cumbersome than assigning the D to one person. When the D is shared, the people involved must clearly define their procedures for arriving at joint decisions. For example, under what conditions do we meet to make decisions? Do we vote? Does the majority rule? Do we need to continue discussing the issue until we all agree? Whatever the mechanism for arriving at decisions, it had better be clearly defined and understood by all or conflict is all but inevitable.

When the Person Who Has It Won't Use It

At times, teams complain of frustration because the person who has the decision-making authority isn't using it. When you are given the D, you have the responsibility to use it and to be held accountable for the results of your decisions. The failure to take risks and make decisions is something I encounter in consulting projects with some regularity. The following case study is an example.

One of the most common problems in teamwork concerns decision making. Let's take a look at your job and identify some areas where starting conversations about the decision-making authority might help you and your team function at a higher level.

Case Study in Avoiding Risky Decisions

I was once asked to consult the president of a company, in part because his wife noticed that he was working longer and longer hours and that he wasn't coming home from work whistling anymore. Normally upbeat, he had become increasingly serious and preoccupied over a period of months. She urged him to take a look at why he didn't seem to be enjoying his work as much as he used to.

Study of the team revealed an interesting finding. The company was a subsidiary of a much larger organization. While the president and his executive team were tasked with running the company, they answered to the board of directors of the parent company. Moreover, they did business in what could be, from time to time, a highly visible and politicized environment. Complaints from the public about the company's services sometimes drew the disapproving attention of the board of directors.

The president had assembled a qualified and capable executive team. However, an interesting thing had slowly happened over time. When very highly visible and risky decisions needed to be made by members of the executive team, they would, in sometimes very subtle ways, pass the issue back to the president to make the decision. I think they may have even done this at times without making a conscious decision to do so. It was just becoming the way they operated. As a result, the president was working harder and longer, and enjoying it less.

After looking at the clarity that "having the D" can bring to this issue, the president went to the post office and got a roll of bulk-mail stickers. Each sticker had a large D on it. Then, when executives would send the president a memo asking for "advice" on a decision—in truth, they were asking him to make the decision—he would slap a D on the memo and return it. He would also add a note asserting that in this area, he had given them the D and he expected them to use it. Sometimes executives would leave his office with D's on their wrists! It was just his way of dramatizing a point. He needed them to understand that as executives they were paid to make decisions—and that is what he was expecting them to do.

Understanding the Consulting Role

If you are affected by a decision and don't have the D, then either you are informed after the decision is made or you serve as a consultant before the decision is made. The consulting role provides the opportunity to participate in the decision-making process, but it is a role that is often misunderstood.

Let's suppose your team at work reports to me. I have been to the latest workshops on participation, and I have been looking for opportunities to get you and the rest of the team more involved in decision making. Suddenly, I see a golden opportunity to do so. In a team meeting, I make an announcement: "I am calling a staff meeting to discuss next year's budget. We have some cuts to make, and how we use our remaining funds will determine what projects we can take on for the coming year."

It is very easy to misunderstand what I am asking for here. You and the rest of the team might be thinking: "We are going to meet. We are going to discuss the budget. Then we are going to make some decisions."

Sorry. Sometimes decision making is not a democratic process. As the leader of this team, I need to make something very clear about the upcoming meeting. This is not an issue that we are going to treat democratically. This is one of those times when I am going to have to retain the D. What I am asking you and your team members to do is act as my consultants before I make my decision. That means I want you to come to the meeting armed with information, recommendations, and a strong point of view about what decisions you think I should make. And I want a meeting in which everyone freely expresses his or her opinion and makes his or her recommendations. In fact, when it comes to budgetary constraints, I expect that some people will feel very strongly about their recommendations and that the discussion may become rather heated at times.

Nevertheless, everyone in the room must come to the meeting with the understanding that this is not one of those decisions that the group is going to make collectively. The meeting is your opportunity to influence my thinking and try to persuade me to make the decision that best suits your particular view of the situation. But, as consultants, you will not be voting. This is one of those times when I feel I must retain the D. You need to understand that in our team meeting I am probably going to be getting two or three very different recommendations about what decisions I should make. I also have my peers giving me their points of view and my boss is certainly giving me hers. My job is to gather all the information I can that will enable me to make the best decision possible. Once I make a decision, my former consultants are obliged to do their best to help make my decision work—regardless of their recommendations on the matter.

One Sunday morning, Lucy said to Charlie Brown, "You know something, Charlie Brown? You win some and you lose some." For several frames Charlie Brown thought this over with furrowed brow. Finally, he said, "That would be nice." Sometimes it can feel that way. It would be nice to win one once in a while. When you don't have the D, you don't always get what you want.

Such is the nature of life in an organization. I was talking to an executive vice president in one of my projects about this. He said:

I am the number two person in my organization, and I consider myself lucky if I get my way half the time. My boss has a grasp on a much bigger picture than I do and is in touch with customers in a way that is impossible for me in my role. There are times I shouldn't get my way. Sometimes I simply don't know enough about what is going on and I need to trust the president to make the right decision.

Having an opportunity to have input in decisions that affect you and your team is a vital way to participate. Creating an environment in which consulting happens freely and easily is both an organizational and an individual challenge. The following exercise will help you identify opportunities to expand consulting on your team.

Exercise 18
Expanding Opportunities for the Consulting Role

- Are you seizing every opportunity to consult your own manager? If not, what is holding you back?

- Are you willing, after reading the chapters on raising issues, to play a more active role in speaking up and making your opinions known?

- Identify at least one example of an opportunity to offer your input on a decision before it is made. How does lack of your input affect the quality of the decision? By what method could you and others offer your input to the decision maker? Take action to make this happen when you have completed reading this book.

For People in Leadership Positions:

- If you lead a team, you have the responsibility to create opportunities for people to consult you and each other freely. In what ways do your employees have the opportunity to consult you? Do you invite this openly or do you depend on people coming through your "open door"?

- List at least three actions you could take to increase the amount of consultation by your team (for example, team meetings to brainstorm problems). Take those actions by the end of the week.

- What have you done to let people know that you want to hear from them? List at least three things you could do to make sure your team understands how important their opinions are to you. Do them by the end of the week.

Making Sure Everyone Is Informed

Sometimes teamwork breaks down because of a simple lack of communication. For example, suppose your management team meets and has long discussions about issues that affect you and your teammates. Finally, decisions are made, and the leader of the management team assumes that the rest of the managers will have the good sense to inform their teams about these decisions and how they will affect them.

You probably know from your own experience that one of the breakdowns in communication happens at the midmanagement or supervisory level. I have seen company presidents dismayed time and again about the degree to which people further down the chain are being kept in the dark about issues and decisions that affect them. These leaders had counted on their management teams to communicate appropriately. Unfortunately, for some managers, communication is not one of their strengths.

It is easy to take the lack of communication personally. The issue itself should be easy to talk about. Teams need to create procedures to ensure that everyone is kept informed. This certainly includes keeping people informed about recent decisions and upcoming issues that directly affect the work they do. But it should also include broader issues of importance to the company as a whole. No one likes being kept in the dark, and making the effort to keep people informed about the company as a whole builds a more involved and committed workforce.

Unfortunately, the lack of communication is sometimes interpreted in highly personalized ways. People may think that management in general or their own manager in particular wants "to keep us in the dark." They may think that management isn't keeping people informed because they don't care about people or because they are withholding bad news and are waiting for the right time to spring it on them. Or they may just reach the conclusion that their management team is inept and incapable of understanding the importance of communication.

When issues are personalized, it is difficult for the people involved to bring them to the table for discussion. Management does not want to hear that they are inept or that they are withholding information from people because they don't care about them. Employees are not likely to even raise a personalized issue for discussion. Professionalizing an issue, on the other hand, can provide the opportunity for it to be rationally discussed and easily resolved.

We need to create procedures to keep everyone up to date on current events in the company. There are many ways of accomplishing this. Regular staff meetings can meet the need. A memo from upper management after team meetings may get the job done. Companies are also experimenting with email and internal web sites as communication tools. The following exercise will help you make sure you are keeping everyone informed.

Creating Participation

You may be fortunate enough to work for a company that is opening up participation in decision making. If so, there are some important distinctions to make about how companies can create participation without the process becoming a mass of unrealistic and unmet expectations.

Exercise 19
Ensuring Timely Access to Information

- List any examples of times when you and/or your team are affected by the lack of timely information.
- Who has the information?

- By what method could that information be made more readily available to those who need it? Take action to see that you get it.
- If you are in a leadership position, ask your staff where they are lacking timely access to the information they need to do their jobs. If any examples are identified, work with the team to devise a method to make sure this situation is remedied.

Driving the "D" out into the Organization

One way to create more participation in decision making is to give away the D wherever possible. There may be many decisions your manager is currently making that you could just as easily make yourself. In fact, making those decisions on your own might make it a lot easier for you to do your job. If you could make the decision, you wouldn't have to find a manager to make that decision, thereby slowing things down. Having the D would also give you more of a sense of ownership and pride in the work you do. So look carefully at your job. Are there places where you don't have the D but feel that you should? If so, there is a conversation with your manager that may be well worth having.

Creating an Open Environment That Encourages Consulting

Another way to create more participation is cultural in nature. It involves management and staff working together to create an environment in which everyone is encouraged to speak his or her mind. This is the way organizations get smarter. It is a way of tapping into the collective intelligence and experience of the people who are closest to the work.

For managers, this means resisting the sometimes overwhelming urge to be brilliant. Managers think they are paid to know things and make decisions. But the simple truth is that if you are a manager, you cannot possibly know everything that is going on in the team you lead—regardless of whether you lead an entire company or a small team of six people. If you will only listen, and if people will only speak up, you will begin to develop a much more informed view of what is going on in your part of the organization.

Great leaders know how important it is to get people to speak up. During World War II, General Douglas MacArthur was noted for asking for input on important decisions. When you are in the military, the patches and insignia on everyone's uniforms create a very clearly defined pecking order. Knowing that military subordinates will often wait to see how the boss feels about something before speaking up, MacArthur would ask the lowest-ranking people at the table what

When everyone participates, organizations get smarter.

they thought. Then he would work his way around the table, asking the highest-ranking people in the room for their opinion last. MacArthur knew very well that the stars on his shoulders gave him the authority and responsibility to make the final decision. Clearly, he had the D. But he also knew he would make a more informed, better-thought-out decision if everyone would openly discuss the matter at hand without letting rank get in the way. Ultimately, he would decide, and everyone would line up behind the decision.

Organizational Benefits of Participatory Decision Making

Organizations all across the country are going to great lengths to create an environment in which people can participate in decision making. They are doing this for two reasons. First, you end up with better decisions when everyone shares his or her point of view. It is like picking up a jewel and looking at it through its many facets. The collective group knowledge is greater than that of any manager, so bringing people in on decisions only makes sense.

There is also another benefit to group involvement in decision making. Not only is the end result a better decision, but people end up supporting the decision with greater enthusiasm if they have been involved in its making. This is true even when decisions don't go the way some individuals on the team hoped they would. If we have been a part of the decision-making process, we are more likely to understand and support a decision than we would be if the same decision had simply been handed to us.

Pitfalls and Misconceptions Regarding Participation

Creating participation makes good business sense. But companies are finding that implementing participation isn't as easy as they had hoped. And if you work in a participatory environment, you may have experienced some disappointments along the way. There are several factors that are creating challenges to the successful implementation of participation in decision making.

The Influence of Personal History

Personal history plays a very important role in how willing people are to jump at the opportunity to participate. Some people have had a lifetime of experiences in which they learned that it is dangerous to be too open around people in authority. We may have learned from bitter experience that disagreement with a boss results in punishment. This can take the form of comments about "negative attitudes" in a performance appraisal. At other times, the punishment is more subtle and interpersonal in nature, with a manager reacting in a way that makes it very clear that disagreement is something that will not be tolerated.

These messages will follow people from company to company. An invitation from a company to participate fully in identifying problems and looking for solutions may sound tempting. After all, most people want to work in an environment in which their voice can be heard and their opinion makes a difference. But some people have a very difficult time trusting the invitation to participate. They are looking for evidence that their manager means what he or she says and will live up to the promise of an open and safe environment.

When people's personal history predisposes them to be wary of management, they will almost certainly find evidence that managers are indeed not to be trusted. Even the best of managers have times when they are distracted and don't listen well. Or they might be under a great deal of pressure to get something done and cut someone short in a conversation. When this kind of thing happens to people who are already looking for evidence of danger, they are likely to withdraw from voluntary participation, with all their fears about people in authority confirmed.

Participation must be **carefully nurtured.**

The Misconception That Participation
Reduces Everything to a Vote

The pursuit of participation sometimes results in things grinding to a halt. This happens when managers and staff fail to make the distinction between the decision-making and consulting roles. Time and again, I have seen teams experience gridlock because they mistakenly assumed that participation meant almost every decision on the team must now be referred to the team.

This results in two predictable consequences. First, managers wind up resisting the company's participatory initiative. Why wouldn't they? Thinking that all decisions must now be served up to the team, they fear that they will be rendered unable to manage the units they are still accountable for leading. And if the manager is truly left with no D, then in fact he or she will be unable to make anything happen without the team's buy-in.

The second thing that happens is that things begin to bog down. If everyone on the team expects to be involved in all of the decision making, the consequences are predictable: there are endless team meetings and debates over how decisions are to be made democratically. The failure to make timely decisions results, as teams get caught up in the pursuit of "consensus," which often gets interpreted as meaning something like, "Until everyone agrees, we have no decision." Not only does this kind of consensus take a long time to reach, it also results in watered-down decisions as proposed alternatives get negotiated into a form that no one will object to.

If you are a member of a team pursuing participation, it is important for you and your teammates to be clear about these aspects of the participation:

Your management has the right—and **sometimes** the responsibility— **to retain** decision-making authority over **certain decisions.**

- The invitation to participate does not mean that management is giving up its right to make decisions.
- Your manager has the right to retain certain D's.
- There will be times when it is more efficient to locate the D with an individual or a subgroup within the team.
- Participation sometimes means having or sharing the D.

- Participation can also mean consulting the decision maker. This means you don't have a vote. What you do have is the invitation to influence the decision maker. This is a valid participatory role.
- You will not get everything you want, even on a participatory team. When you don't get what you want, it does not mean that participation is a sham. It just means that you didn't get what you want.

The right to reserve decision-making authority to management is something that is important for managers and staff alike to bear in mind. Sometimes it makes no sense to defer a particular decision to the team. Imagine yourself as a patient in a hospital suffering from severe chest pains and shortness of breath. How would you feel if you were to overhear the doctor saying the following? "This patient is having a heart attack, and I think we should start medication to prevent the patient from going into full cardiac arrest. Let's do a forced-choice voting process to make sure that all team members are in agreement with this course of action." Obviously, you would want to know that someone in that room is in charge and that care will be delivered now, not after the team finally agrees on a course of action.

Now most decisions facing a team are not as dramatic as decisions faced by an emergency health care team. Nevertheless, there will definitely be times when efficiency is served by locating the decision-making authority with a manager or some other individual team member. Group participation in decision making takes time and should be reserved only for certain kinds of decisions.

In crisis, the need for speed may call for consolidation of authority and less participation.

If you are a manager, creating participation does not mean that you are required to yield the D on every decision. Participation does not have to lead to endless meetings and a team paralyzed by the inability to reach consensus on every decision. The management team has every right to reserve certain decisions for management, such as decisions that cut across department lines or decisions affecting personnel. You may also consolidate the authority in a manager or delegate it to some other individual when prompt action is required, making consideration of the decision by a team impractical.

If you are a team member, participation will open up your involvement in decisions that affect how you do your work. Sometimes you will have the D. If there are times you think you should have the D but don't, ask for it. Other times, you will be making recommendations to the decision maker. When companies are in the early stages of creating participation, some people set themselves up for disappointment by expecting to have or share the D in almost every decision affecting their work. But this is not a very practical way to run a business. Sometimes you will have the D, sometimes you won't.

Some People Don't Want to Participate

Participation requires that all employees show up to work "with their thinking caps on," as one of my teachers used to put it. Working on a participatory team requires that everyone play an active role in identifying problems and looking for ways to improve how things get done. It also requires people to take responsibility for starting conversations that make things happen. Waiting passively to be asked is not an acceptable participatory stance.

Taking an active role in work is new to some people. It may feel risky to speak up in meetings. It can be frightening to take the initiative in a conversation to resolve a problem or suggest that the team try a new way of doing things that might be more efficient. As a result, some people hold back from participating fully, even though they might wish they had the courage to do so. If you are one of those people, take heart. The following chapters on communication strategies will provide you with ways of taking the conversational initiative. Pay close attention to the suggestions on how to prepare for these conversations. A little thought put into the conversation ahead of time can help you take careful aim and avoid shooting yourself in the foot.

There are also people who don't like participatory environments because they just don't like putting that much of themselves into their work. Their motto seems to be, "Don't ask me to think. Just tell me what to do." If you were one of those people, you probably wouldn't be bothering to read this book. Even if your manager asked you to read it, you probably would have found a way to avoid it before you got this far. So my comments here are directed to those who have the misfortune to work with teammates who don't like to put much of themselves into their work.

If you find that you have people on your team who are not pulling their own weight, you, too, should read the upcoming chapters on communication strategies carefully. On a participatory team, you don't have the luxury of waiting for management to take care of something. As you probably know from previous experience, waiting can be a futile strategy anyway. Sometimes managers don't pay enough attention to notice that they have a team member who is not performing at the same level as the rest of the team. And even if they do notice, some managers are reluctant to take action.

So if you have a teammate who is not fully engaged with the rest of the team, it is up to you to have a conversation that might make the difference with him or her. You will find the chapters on raising issues to be very helpful in this regard. For now, do a quick assessment of your team. Is everyone pulling together or is there someone whose mind seems to be somewhere else? This person may even angrily reject the invitation to participate fully, stating that "they don't pay me enough to think. I just do what I am told." If you work with someone like that, you have a real opportunity to put the coming communication strategies to the test.

Personal Benefits of Participation

Companies often start participatory efforts in the pursuit of quality improvements in their products and services. They are also interested in the cost savings available through the reduction of waste, errors, and inefficiency. So what is in it for you? Plenty.

Having More Say over the Daily Details of Your Work

One of the most obvious benefits of participating fully is expanding your influence over the day-to-day decisions that affect your work. Numerous studies of job satisfaction find that people want to be in on things and to have a greater sense of control over the details that affect them on the job. Participation gives you the opportunity to create more of a sense of autonomy and control over your work.

But you have to ask for it. Never forget that your management is not as close to the work as you are. Do not assume that they know what is happening for you on the job. They won't know where you should play a greater role in making the many decisions that affect your ability to get your job done. They simply do not see things as clearly as you do. How could they? You are the one doing your job. Even your direct supervisor may know less about the particulars of your job than you think he or she should. This means that it is absolutely essential for you to be willing to speak up. Look for opportunities to participate more fully and start the conversations necessary to make it happen.

Participation Results in Higher Levels of Personal Satisfaction

People who work in participatory environments report a higher level of engagement with their work. They also find work more satisfying. I will never forget a conversation I had with a member of the self-directed work team in a bank. The bank's president had decided that the people who worked in the branches should not have to have a supervisor. "After all," he said, "these people are raising families. They vote. Some have given years of their lives to our country in military service. We shouldn't have to manage them. They should be able to manage themselves." Moving toward self-directed branch teams would also free up the branch managers. They could then pay more attention to the development of new business.

The branch teams had been at this for some time, with all the predictable confusion and learning that occurs when teams are asked to do everything for themselves that their supervisors used to do. I was talking to a young woman in her mid-twenties about her reaction to the changes occurring in her job. "When I am at home on weekends," she said, "I think about my job now." She went on to explain:

I don't mean that in a bad way. It is just that now I like thinking about my work and how we can work together to get things done. This is new to me. I used to work to pay my bills. But now that we are more in control of our own days at the branch, I find it is much more satisfying to do a good job.

Do you want to find more satisfaction in your work? Step forward and look for ways to participate more fully. Get involved. Take the initiative. And do so freely, without worrying about whether they are paying you enough to take this kind of ownership of the job. The personal payoffs will come in the form of greater control over your work and the satisfaction that comes with making a difference.

Chapter Eight

Conversations Dying to Happen

Taking action requires two sets of skills: thinking skills and conversational skills. Up to now, we have been developing thinking skills. We have been discussing the world of work and the tangled interpersonal relationships we find there. We have looked at the two relationships we have with our co-workers and how important it is to keep our personal and professional perspectives straight, especially in times of conflict. We have also studied guidelines for working relationships and diagnosing conflict—goal, roles, and procedures. Finally, we have examined the three roles you can play in any decision that affects you directly: you make the decision, you consult the decision maker before the decision is made, or you are informed afterward.

But knowledge without action is useless.

Communication—the Source of Working Relationships

It can be argued that the heart of working together is communication. Everything you do all day long is the result of communication. Some of it is written; some of it occurs in meetings when groups of people get together. But the bulk of our communication at work happens one on one—one person talking to another about what needs to get done and how they are going to work together to make it happen. Most of the time, our communication works pretty well. But what happens when it doesn't? The real test of our teamwork is what happens when we are in conflict.

Every time you are in conflict, you are faced with a choice: Are you going to take this conflict personally, or are you going to trust in the other person's intentions and proceed to professionalize the issue? I wish that this could be an easy choice for us to make, but it isn't. It is so easy to jump to conclusions, yield to our emotions, and take conflict personally. And it all happens in the heat of the moment, almost without our recognizing what is happening to us at the time.

Conflict and Anger

Think about the last time you got angry with someone at work. If you are like most people, you probably have more than enough to do on any given day at work. You work under pressure. You want to get the job done and get it done right. Then something happens in the middle of an already busy day. You discover that your boss made some important decisions affecting your work but neglected to tell you about it. A co-worker failed to do something you were expecting him or her to do, and now you're stuck with yet another task that must be done by the end of the day. Or someone from another department puts up a roadblock that is going to complicate an already complicated day.

Nothing derails clear thinking and **open communication** faster than **anger** given **free rein.**

After our conversation about personalizing versus professionalizing, it would be nice if we could be perfectly disciplined every time something like this happens to disrupt our day:

Golly, my boss failed to tell me that our goals had changed, and I have just spent the last four hours doing the wrong thing and now I am hopelessly behind. I will never get out of here on time tonight. Oh, well. I guess we just need to talk about creating a procedure to make sure that I get the information I need in order to do my work. There is, after all, nothing personal going on here....

It would be nice if we could be that disciplined in our thinking. Unfortunately, theory is one thing, but putting theory into practice on a daily basis can be quite something else, especially when we are under pressure.

So what happens to most of us when we experience frustration on the job? We may suddenly find ourselves in a swirl of angry thoughts and emotions:

That stupid idiot! How am I supposed to know what is going on unless he tells me? Of all the lamebrained things he's done, this one really ticks me off. Now I'll be working overtime while that bozo gets to go to the ball game tonight. Man, would I ever like to give Mister We-Are-All-in-This-Together-and-Communication-Makes-It-Work a piece of my mind!

And the more we think about it, the angrier we get. This is one of the unfortunate consequences of personalizing. Once we get on a roll, we can end up very angry, sometimes much angrier than the occasion calls for.

I sometimes wonder if we experience a certain perverse satisfaction in anger. We get to rant and rave, all the while making some other person or situation the cause of all of our problems. We may even do a little unloading. We may already be tired and frustrated, and this incident becomes an occasion to let all our feelings come pouring out. This can even feel good, especially when we are gossiping with our teammates and we have a good "group gripe" going. We end up further reinforcing each other's notions about how screwed up this place is and about how poorly we are being treated. This is a conversation that is going to get us nowhere in a hurry.

When we are angry, we need to think first, then speak. We are about to look at a preparation strategy that provides a method for doing just that. This chapter will give you a tool that will help you sort out your thoughts, set your personal feelings aside for the moment, and get ready to professionalize the conversation.

Conflict and Fear

For some people, the response to conflict is fear rather than anger. To understand this, recall our conversation about personal history. Some people learn, through a series of harsh life experiences, that conflict is dangerous and to be avoided at all costs. They may have a long history of harsh treatment by people in authority. Parents and teachers may have had little tolerance for disagreement. Or, as is often the case, they may have worked in companies where, in fact, disagreement with anyone in authority was severely received. Even someone with good intentions and a legitimate complaint might have been sanctioned for having a "bad attitude" or, that all-time favorite, "not being a good team player."

When people with this kind of history run into problems at work, they do their best to maintain a low profile. There may be things that are bothering them, but the last

The **"team player"** may have a history of being **hammered into submission.**

thing they want to do is rock the boat. They have learned that the best thing to do when something bothers them is nothing at all. They work on, sometimes in wounded silence. They don't realize the solution to their problem might be just one conversation away from happening—if only they had the courage to speak up.

Some people have tried to deal with conflict openly in the past but have had bad experiences doing so. In an earlier time in their career, they may have tried to raise issues and deal with problems head-on. Unfortunately, lacking the skills to do this appropriately, they may have lashed out emotionally. This often produces a very negative reaction, one in which the substance of the issue itself gets lost. The attention shifts to a discussion of how inappropriately they are behaving and, in extreme cases, a warning is given or implied that any further incidents of this kind will be dealt with harshly.

In these instances, people mistakenly conclude that they are better off if they keep their mouth shut. They make a decision to withdraw from any further discussions that are tinged with conflict. They will sometimes justify their stance with the reassurance that "people around here are threatened by strong women," or "my boss is threatened by assertive people." What gets lost is the opportunity to learn something important about themselves: they may be talking about legitimate issues but doing so in a way that is alienating them from the rest of the team. Anytime I hear people talk about other people being threatened by them, I almost always discover that these individuals are very inappropriate in their dealings with others. People don't avoid them because they are "powerful." People avoid them because they are unpleasant to work with.

If you think that people are **intimidated** by your **"power,"** take a closer look. It just **might be possible** that you are **not** very **pleasant** to work with.

When people become highly fearful or anxious when faced with conflict, they become reluctant to take action. They are often very bright, capable people with a point of view that would be well worth hearing. Unfortunately, they do not speak up. When they do, their approach may be so tentative that they fail to make their case with any power. Their resolve to stand up for themselves and their opinions crumbles at the first sign of resistance.

Like angry people, fearful people need a preparation strategy for dealing with conflict, though for a different reason. It is hard to think on your feet when you are anxious. Thoughts become jumbled and tongues become tied. The power to reason clearly takes flight. I have seen very bright, capable people all but dissolve when asked to defend an idea, especially when they are grilled skeptically by someone with more authority.

The preparation strategy we are about to discuss is not a cure-all. It will certainly help the highly anxious person prepare his or her case ahead of time. He or she can even practice putting it into words with a co-worker. Preparation helps people belay the fear that they are going to get confused and forget what they wanted to say in the middle of the conversation. Of course, they will still have to get up the courage to actually raise the issue for discussion. The conversational strategies offered in the next chapter will help considerably.

If Talk Is So Important, Why Do We Stop?

Let's take it as a given for the moment that teamwork comes down to an endless series of conversations about work and how to get things done. I am willing to bet that most of us have had times when there was a conversation we knew we needed to have to make something happen at work. We went to work with the resolve to talk to our boss about a problem or to fix some glitch in coordination with a co-worker. Just about the time we approached the person to talk, however, we stopped short of actually doing it, thinking perhaps, "Well, maybe tomorrow would be a better day."

Is this true for you, too? Have there been times when you have stopped short of talking to someone, even though you knew you needed to have this conversation to get something important accomplished? We all know the only way to get there from here is through a conversation. Yet, on some days with some people, we stop short of actually talking to someone.

We stop talking for many reasons. Sometimes we stop because we anticipate that the conversation is going to end in a battle. In fact, we may have had previous experiences with this person, and we've learned that talk is not only fruitless, it is frustrating and stressful. So we stop to avoid unpleasant conflict.

Some hold back because they think a conversation with someone will be pointless. This person rarely listens to anyone. Why should this time be any different? Others hold back because they feel unprepared and believe that they need to think the issue through for a bit longer. No one wants to look bad. The person we need to approach may be a senior manager. This individual may be scary to approach because of her position, or she may have an interpersonal style that makes her difficult to approach.

I worked with Glen, an executive vice president of a nationally prominent bank, a few years ago. He was one of the brightest executives I've known over the years. In fact, his keen intelligence made him somewhat intimidating. He was unhappy because even his executive staff were sometimes reluctant to deal with him. My interviews revealed that people would work for days on a report or proposal, very carefully trying to catch every detail. Yet when they presented it to Glen, he would pick up the report, read it quickly, and start to probe the presenters on the one detail of the project that they might not have thought about. Glen's intentions were good. He wanted to provide his staff with coaching. They, on the other hand, experienced the moment as, "Once again I am standing here looking stupid in front of my boss when I thought I was prepared."

Some people shut down for a long time if you make them feel stupid or exposed.

No one wants to look stupid. Even if executives work hard at being open and supportive, there will be people who have a great deal of difficulty speaking up to them, especially about anything even remotely controversial. And so it is that they walk around with unspoken issues that need to be heard, issues that could make a difference for the company. If you are like the rest of us, there are times you stop short of starting conversations you know you need to have. The following exercise will help you analyze why you do this.

Making Conversations Happen

Making things happen takes disciplined thinking and, sometimes, courage. But without taking action and starting conversations to make things happen, nothing happens. Everything stays in place.

Exercise 20
The Costs and Gains of Avoiding Conversations

- Do you tend to avoid conversations with particular people? What is it about these particular people that you are avoiding?

- What price are you paying for avoiding these conversations?

- What do you gain by avoiding these conversations? For example, you may get to avoid the discomfort of disagreeing with someone in authority or avoid the risk of a conversation that might result in a heated disagreement.

- Reflect for a moment on the costs and gains of avoidance. Sure, there is a short-term payoff. But is it worth the price you will pay if your concerns are never addressed?

I can remember a demonstration in one of my high school science classes. On his desk, the instructor placed a beaker of fluid that he described as a "supersaturated solution." That meant that the solution had absorbed as much salt as it possibly could and still remain a fluid. Then he held up a tiny crystal that he described as a "seed crystal." He dropped the crystal into the solution, and the solution turned into a solid. It looked like magic to me, but I have come to think of this phenomenon as a metaphor for the workplace. Sometimes, as an outsider, I look at teams and see that all the conditions are in place for some change to occur. Sometimes all it takes to make something dramatic happen is for one person to have the courage to say, "I will be the seed crystal. I will be the catalyst for change. I am going to make something happen." Sometimes, with careful preparation and an approach to the right person, change is just a conversation away.

But if you are going to step forward and make something happen, you want to do it intelligently. This is especially true when the issues are tough and your emotions are running high. You need to carefully think through what you are going to say and how you are going to say it. Otherwise, you may not get quite the reaction you had hoped for. Making things happen is best thought of as a series of steps:

- *Remind yourself not to take things so personally.* Are you angry, frustrated, or intimidated by the person you need to talk to? Remind yourself not to take things so personally. The important thing to do is focus on the job that needs to be done. Yielding to your emotions will only interfere with your ability to think clearly and speak persuasively. It is quite likely that the other people involved are doing what they are doing for reasons that make perfect sense to them. They are not doing it because they want to ruin your day. Take a deep breath and remind yourself that there is nothing personal going on here. If the issue that concerns you is having an impact on the job you're doing, there is a way to talk about this without letting your emotions get in the way.

- *Prepare—don't act in the heat of the moment.* Following the preparation strategy we are about to explore together, think through the issue carefully. The more important the issue, the more it deserves a little time put into thinking about it so that you can present your case as persuasively as possible.
- *Act!* While preparation is important, don't let it become a way of avoiding dealing with the issue. The next chapter will present a conversational strategy for raising issues. Review it. You may be about to start a conversation that has been dying to happen for a long time.

The Value of Thinking Before Speaking

When a conversation doesn't go well for me, one of two things has usually happened. I may not have thought the issue through very well, and in the middle of the conversation, it became all too apparent that I didn't know what I was talking about. Usually this causes no lasting damage—other than embarrassment—as I scramble to retrieve something of value from the conversation without losing any more face than I already have. Sometimes I choose the unfortunate strategy of continuing to talk until I think of something to say. I usually just wind up digging myself into a deeper hole.

The other way a conversation might not go well is much more hazardous to my relationships and my credibility. Looking back over my working history, some of my worst moments occurred when I took an emotional dive into the deep end. Some people may be able to think clearly in the heat of anger, but I am not one of them. I may start out with the intention of discussing an issue professionally, but if my emotions rise, I will soon find myself saying some stupid and hurtful things.

If you are like me, here is what happens next. When I go to bed that night, I replay the conversation over and over in my mind—only this time I am absolutely brilliant! I imagine myself saying something. Then the other person says, "Gee, Bob, I hadn't thought of that." Then I say something else, and the person replies, "Bob, I am simply blown away by the force of your logic." Then I say the final thing I need to say, and the other person replies, "Bob, you were right all along. What can I possibly do to make up for the grievous wrong I have done to you?"

This imaginary conversation goes exactly the way I would like to see it go. But something else happens as well. Reflecting back over the real incident, I realize that, in the heat of the moment, I said some stupid things that I wish I had never said. In the middle of some conversations, I have had the experience of saying something and instantly wishing that a sharp intake of breath could suck the words right back into my mouth.

It's easy to think of the perfect thing to say...about six hours too late.

Something else happens as I replay the conversation over and over again in my head. I start thinking of any number of things that I wish I had said. Some of these new arguments and points may be very good ones.

Unfortunately, I am thinking of them hours too late for them to do any good. Spending a few minutes preparing to raise issues can make all the difference in the outcome. This is especially true when you need to talk about difficult issues that carry an emotional load for you or the other person involved.

Using the preparation strategy we'll discuss in the coming pages will help you organize your thoughts and know exactly what you are going to say. This is a confidence builder, especially if the person you need to approach can be a bit intimidating for you to deal with. You will know that you have a plan of action to guide you through the conversation.

If you are emotionally stirred up over the issue, preparation will give you time to take a deep breath and think about the situation more professionally. You will have a better chance of reining in emotions that might otherwise derail the conversation. Acting rashly can do lasting damage to your professional credibility and your relationship with the other person.

Gathering your thoughts before you act may be good stress management —and career preservation— strategy.

You may even discover that the issue isn't worth raising. If you follow the preparation steps carefully, you will be forced to think more objectively about an issue that may be driving you crazy personally. You may discover that you are not able to marshal a forceful and persuasive presentation of your case. If so, you may be well served to take another look at why this issue is bothering you so much. Is it really a professional issue that deserves the other person's attention? Or is this something that is related to a personal preference of yours but really cannot be argued persuasively as a professional issue?

For example, you may work on a job that requires staffing seven days a week. You knew that when you took the job. Now you find that you don't like working weekends and you are low on the seniority list. Whining and complaining to your supervisor about this will get you nowhere. It will also be very difficult for you to present a persuasive case to convince your boss that someone else should work on weekends to let you off the hook. You will either have to be patient until your length of tenure on the job earns you a better schedule or you will have to take another look at your fit for this job.

Some issues are highly complex. Thinking through an issue carefully may be the only way you have a chance to be credible. It will give you time to talk to other people for their suggestions. It will give you time to do a bit of necessary research. The last thing you want to do is launch into a complicated suggestion, only to discover that your ideas are coming across as half-baked because you haven't done your homework.

Some conversations are going to be uncomfortable, no matter how much preparation you put into them.

A Caution Regarding Preparation

Don't let your "need to be prepared" be an excuse for not taking action. While preparation is indeed important, for some people it can become a justification for not acting: "I'm not ready yet. I need to give this just a bit more thought." What you are really doing is putting the conversation off until you are "comfortable" with approaching the other person. Unfortunately, there will be times when you will never feel completely comfortable about raising a particular issue for discussion. Raising an issue can be an act of personal courage and an expression of your commitment to the job. The topic you want to discuss might be an emotional mine field. Preparation will help, but the land mines will still be there. You will still need to have the courage to act.

There is another reason why people are slow in taking action. Some people are extremely detail oriented. When they think an issue through, their thinking may be far more detailed and precise than is necessary. If you are one of these highly detailed people, you may not even realize it and think that this doesn't apply to you. Your thinking is very detailed because that is how you see the world and that is the way things work for you. However, at some point, you have to say enough is enough and take action. Otherwise these mental detours can consume time when you could be taking action.

Outline for Raising Issues

When you are faced with an important discussion to resolve a problem or make a suggested change, the Raising Issues Worksheet that is presented at the end of this chapter will be a helpful tool. It will guide you through a sequence of topics to consider as you get ready for your discussion. This worksheet is a brainstorming tool. Use it like that. Dump out ideas as they occur to you. Don't worry about organization—you will take care of that when you transfer this information to your Raising Issues Discussion Form, which we will talk about in the next chapter.

You will note that the worksheet has four sections: Problem, Impact, Requests, and Benefits. We will look at each section of the preparation sheet in detail.

Problem

You may start out with a highly personalized view of the situation. For example, you may feel the problem is obvious: right now, you are working with a vain, self-centered jerk who doesn't care about anyone but himself and his own interests.

Al is the manager of a team whose work must be closely coordinated with you and your team if you are going to be successful in getting your job done. Lately, things have not been going well at all. You and Al held a joint planning meeting in which you discussed coordinating the activities of your respective teams.

It is only days after your planning session, and Al is already making decisions that are making things very difficult for you and your team. First, he obviously—or so it seems to you—cares only about the priorities he and his team have to meet. He is making decisions about resource allocation that are advantageous to his group but result in delays and frustration for your team. Furthermore, he is making these decisions without consulting you or even informing you in time for you to make the necessary adjustments. "All this talk from our division manager about one for all and all for one," you think. "What a crock!" Over the last couple of days, you have begun to wonder if Al is just trying to look good, even if it is at the expense of his fellow managers like yourself. Is he deliberately trying to undermine you? Is there a competitive thing going on here?

Your heated assessments of other people have no place in workplace conversations. First of all, you may very well be wrong. The other person is probably doing what makes sense to him, given his understanding of the situation and the agreements he has with you. But let us suppose you are accurate, that Al really is deliberately violating your agreements with him and undermining you so that he will look good. Even if that were true, what would happen if you accused him of it? He would probably get defensive and respond with some accusations of his own. The conversation between the two of you would very quickly devolve into a heated argument. In the end, little progress would be made toward resolving the problem. Your staff would be in the same fix they were in to begin with. Only now your relationship with Al would be further damaged, making teamwork between your departments all the harder to come by.

Your assessments of the other person's **character** or intentions have **no place** in business **conversations.**

If you are going to raise this issue for discussion, you had better spend some time professionalizing it. Breakdowns in teamwork and communication are to be expected. You want to be able to describe the problem by using the guidelines for working relationships we discussed in earlier chapters. That means describing an issue as emerging from some ambiguity or disagreement regarding goals, roles, and procedures.

In this example with Al, clearly there are some procedural issues afoot. You apparently have no procedure to ensure that Al will inform you in a timely way regarding any decisions he is making that will affect your staff. Moreover, there may be a need to talk about roles in decision making. Right now he is exercising the D without any input from you. Perhaps this issue can best be described as a problem in how decisions get made, indicating the need for you to be able to consult Al on certain decisions, to provide him with information about your team before he makes those decisions.

Your ability to describe the issue in language that emphasizes teamwork and the job you want to get done is critical. Using more objective and less judgmental terms is the first step in defusing the defensiveness that so often occurs when we reach out to resolve conflicts at work. Al is much more likely to be open to a conversation that begins with your concern about your mutual roles in decision making and the lack of procedures to ensure that you and your team are kept informed. Your assessments of Al's character are not relevant. Attacking his character or intentions is a surefire way to produce an uncomfortable and unproductive moment for both of you.

When you raise an issue for discussion, you want to be able to make clear to the other person that it is not personal. You are not raising this issue *because* you are angry—even if you *are* angry. You are not raising the issue so that the other person will do something that will make you feel better—even though that might be one outcome of finding a solution. You are not raising this issue because you think the other person is a jerk—even though he or she might be one of those rare, genetically predetermined, came-out-of-the-womb-and-started-telling-the-nurses-how-to-do-their-jobs jerks.

The one and only reason you are taking up this person's time is because some condition exists that is having a negative impact on the job you need to get done. That is why you spent so much time carefully describing the issue in professional terms. Some people start conversations by telling the other person not to take what they are going to say personally. Then they proceed to attack the other person and his or her behavior in ways that are guaranteed to produce defensiveness and an argument.

> **"Don't take this** personally, but..." **is almost** always followed by a **highly personal attack.**

Impact

After describing the issue using professional, objective terms, you need to describe why this situation is of concern to you: it is having a negative impact on the job.

If you are getting ready to raise an issue, you are more than likely getting ready to talk to someone over whom you have no direct authority.

In others words, you do not have the power to force him or her to do anything. You may be getting ready for a conversation with a member of your team. It may be someone from another department who is in some way causing a problem for you. Or your conversation may involve someone who is your senior in terms of authority. It may be your own boss or perhaps a senior-level manager from some other part of the company. When thinking about how you will convey the impact of the issue, here are some considerations.

Getting Ready to Be Persuasive

In this conversation, you cannot mandate the outcome. If you were approaching someone who worked for you, you could, if absolutely necessary, try to force compliance with your request. But today's managers are well aware of the limits of their ability to force their staff to do anything for very long. So if you are entering into a conversation in which you have little or no authority to make something happen, what then should you rely on for a conversation to produce a positive outcome? In a word—persuasion.

One of your most important goals in preparation is to get ready to persuade the other person that the problem you are describing is having an impact that must be taken seriously. If the other person does not respond positively to your request, it may be because he or she does not take the issue seriously. The person may not see the impact of this situation on the job you are all being paid to accomplish.

So you need to prepare your arguments now, ahead of time, rather than try to think of good things to say during the conversation itself. If the other person doesn't think the problem deserves attention or change, then you need to be ready to persuade him or her that, in fact, it does. In your preparation, think of every impact statement you can possibly dredge up regarding this issue. How is this situation affecting costs? What about service to your customers? Is the situation having an impact on employee morale? What about the company's reputation in the marketplace or your mutual teams' reputation within the company? Is the problem having an impact on quality or efficiency?

You may work for a company that has gone to a great deal of effort and expense to create a vision statement and share it with everyone in the company. This kind of organizational development work varies widely in format. Your company's leadership may have shared their long-range goals for the company. They may have published a mission statement.

Some companies publish a statement of corporate values or guiding principles that might address the quality of the work you do or the kind of corporate culture that is being held up as the ideal.

If your leadership has gone to the trouble of sharing their hopes for the company, this can be a great place to look for impact statements when preparing to raise an issue. The situation may be inconsistent with the accomplishment of the company's long-term goals. The problem may be undermining the accomplishment of the company's mission. Perhaps the quality of teamwork is out of step with the company's stated values.

Remember the last time you lay awake in bed at night replaying a conversation that didn't go well? Remember thinking of all those brilliant things you wish you had thought to say at the time? The preparation you are doing now *before* raising the issue will help you avoid the experience of thinking of that perfect point you thought of *after* the conversation. So spend whatever time it takes on this step. If appropriate, approach other people who may be experiencing the same situation. See if they can think of any impact statements that you haven't yet thought of.

Thinking About What's in It for the Other Person

Spend some time thinking about how this situation might be experienced by the other person. What are the payoffs for the other person in the situation as it exists today? How can you persuade the other person that paying attention to your concerns is in his or her best interest as well? At the very least, the other person is presumed to be as committed to the company's success and service to customers as you are.

Separating Impact from Personal Preference

Focusing on impact on the job eliminates mere personal preference from the conversation. As you focus on impact statements, you may discover that an issue of concern to you might not be worth talking about after all. I will never forget working with a group in a team development project. We were having a discussion about the importance of being able to point to the impact on the job. From the back of the room, I heard someone say, "White socks." The rest of the team laughed. The

Choose your battles carefully. Some **issues** are **not important** enough to bring to the table **for discussion.**

comment seemed far removed from the brilliant point I thought I was making. I asked what he meant. "I am always bugging people about wearing white socks to work," he said.

But I've been sitting here trying to come up with some impact on the job and I can't think of a single reason why they shouldn't be able to wear white socks. The color of their socks has absolutely no impact on the job. I guess this is a personal quirk of mine and I'm going to have to let go of it.

This is a great example of the importance of thinking about the impact of any situation that is bothering you at work. In this situation, the color of a person's socks had no job impact. But suppose the situation involved someone who was involved in public relations, including appearances on television to represent the company. You could make an argument that white socks and an elegant blue suit don't make a good match. But this can be even more persuasively stated. The combination of white socks and a business suit might leave some people with the impression that the wearer is unpolished and unprofessional. The wearer is representing the company. People might end up making some unfortunate judgments about the company, based on their reactions to the company representative's mode of dress. In this circumstance, the color of someone's socks can become an issue that can be professionalized.

At the risk of belaboring my point, I'll say this one more time: *your personal feelings are not relevant when talking about work-related problems.* Leave your personal feelings out of this stage of your preparation. Don't misunderstand me, I am not saying that how you feel is not important. Your work is, of course, very important to you. But you are getting ready to be persuasive and to make your points as a professional who is committed to doing a great job. Don't go to your boss and tell her that you are unhappy and then ask her do to something so you will feel better. She may just send you to a stress management workshop.

In personal relationships, as opposed to professional ones, the assumption is that the other person *cares* how you feel. Stating feelings directly is a way of building intimacy. Talking about how you feel about something is very appropriate when discussing something that is bothering you in a personal relationship. But most of your conversations at work are not about intimacy and closeness—or at least, in my opinion, they shouldn't be. Most of the time we should be talking about what it is going to take to get the job done. The traditional assertion model of communication focuses on feelings. This sets a person up for conversations that can spiral out of control, especially when the issue at stake is one that carries a heavy emotional charge.

Some of you may see my approach to workplace conflict as "lacking authenticity" or "encouraging people not to own their feelings." Telling someone you are outraged at some decision they made may be "authentic," but it also can be a bad career move. I am not encouraging you to keep your mouth shut and put up with something that is bothering you. Speak up. But do so intelligently. At work, this means being willing to set your personal feelings aside and focus on the job that needs to be done. This section of your preparation will help you be open and direct with your co-workers, but in a way that is more appropriate on the job.

There *is* an appropriate time and place for talking about your feelings at work. We will be talking about strategies for doing so in the last section of this book.

Impact Statements

Let's go back to our friend Al, who I introduced earlier in this chapter. If you are getting ready to approach him about the problem I described, your brainstorming of impact statements might include the following:

Don't be reckless. Resolutely "taking a stand" can damage your credibility—perhaps even your career.

- The lack of information about Al's decisions is costing the company money. My staff members are left in the dark. They will have to go back and redo work once they are aware of Al's decision.
- My lack of input means that he is making decisions that could be based on a broader understanding of the impact on other departments.
- Some of the frustration my staff members are experiencing is spilling over into their relationships with Al's staff. They are becoming irritated with "those people over in that department who are causing us so much trouble."
- We have a corporate value emphasizing cross-department collaboration. Making decisions without input from my department is inconsistent with that value.

- One of our values emphasizes efficiency. Having to do work over again once we discover what Al's department is doing is certainly not consistent with that value.
- Our corporate vision statement talks about creating a great place to work. Lack of information is causing a level of unnecessary frustration that is having an impact on my staff's job satisfaction.
- Our mutual boss has been asking me about the high costs within our division. If he realizes what a poor job we are doing in coordinating the efforts of our teams, we are both going to end up looking bad.

I could list more ideas about impact statements but I think you get the idea. You will see how valuable this kind of preparation can be in the next chapter.

No one likes **complaints.** Always bring a specific **request, suggestion,** or **solution** to the table.

Requests

This may seem obvious, but I feel it is important to say anyway: *don't go into this conversation without knowing what you want from the other person*. Time and again I have heard managers complain about this. "People keep coming to me with problems and complaints. I just wish they would come to me with solutions." Don't think that what you want will be obvious to the other person once you have described the problem and its impact.

A request is something that the other person can say yes or no to. Go into your conversation ready to make a clear request of the other person. This usually involves something you want the other person to do, such as granting you the resources you need to complete a particular project. For example, you may be requesting the authority to make decisions (the "D") regarding the expenditure of funds up to a certain limit. Or you may be asking for the nod to either start doing something new or stop doing something you are currently doing.

Sometimes you may be absolutely stumped about what request to make. You may, for example, be concerned about a problem that finds its source further "upstream" in the workflow. A certain team does one aspect of a task and passes it along to your team for the next phase of the work. Continuing problems in the work that team is doing are forcing your team to have to spend time making corrections in the work already done before they can go on to do their own work. You may not know what the solution might be. You just know that there is a problem. In this case, your request might be that you and the other manager schedule a joint team meeting so that everyone can sit at the same table, review the situation, and find a solution to the problem. Note that your request isn't offering a specific solution, but you are at least proposing an action that will ultimately lead to a solution.

You may think you are ready to make a specific request. You have thought the situation through, and you think your request can be clearly stated and easily understood. If it is appropriate for you to do so, try your request out on a co-worker before you approach the real conversation. Ask your co-worker to restate your request, using his or her own words. You may discover that your co-worker is unable to follow your request well enough to restate it. If so, you need to do some work on clarifying your request before you get involved in the real thing.

Benefits

This is the easiest part of your preparation. List some of the benefits if the other person says yes to your request. If you are able to eliminate or reduce the factors you pointed out in the impact statements, the benefits are obvious. Be sure to think of at least one benefit that is directly of interest to the person you will be talking to. It may come in handy, as you will see in the next chapter.

In our ongoing preparation for a conversation with Al, we might add the following benefits to our worksheet:

- Solving this problem will reduce costs in that my team won't have to redo its work to adjust for Al's decisions.
- We will reduce the friction between our two teams.
- Both of us will avoid the risk of looking bad to our boss by doing a better job of coordinating the efforts of our two teams.

Before you get into this conversation, think about what you will do if you are unable to reach an agreement that meets your needs. Remember—you don't always get what you want. Sometimes you will have done everything right. You were prepared. You raised your issue professionally. The other person, however, still said no to your request. Such is the nature of life in organizations. You gave it your best shot, and it didn't go the way you wanted. Congratulate yourself for trying and move on.

There may be other times, however, when you feel you cannot let go of your concerns that easily. For example, you may feel that a particular situation is having a severe impact on costs or on employee morale. In your judgment, the situation must be addressed. Before going into this conversation, be sure that you are clear about what you will do next if this conversation fails to reach a satisfactory conclusion.

You might have a couple of possible responses in mind. Suppose Al just doesn't agree with your arguments about being consulted before he makes his decisions. You might want to be prepared to say something like the following: "I had hoped that you and I could find a solution to this issue on our own. However, I think the situation is so serious that I cannot let it stand as it is. I would like to take this to our manager for her opinion. Are you willing to join me in that conversation?"

You might be prepared to take a less aggressive stance in the event of a negative answer. You might say, "Al, I understand your reluctance to make any changes in decision making at this time. However, I want you to know that the next time this issue causes my team a delay, I will come back to you with more information and another attempt to resolve this problem."

Give your boss an **ultimatum** and you may get an **opportunity** to polish your **job-seeking skills.**

Never paint yourself into a corner with a threat. Some people make the mistake of presenting an ultimatum to their boss: "Either give me what I am asking for or I will quit." Don't make this kind of threat unless you are in fact ready to walk. These kinds of threats sometimes are made in the heat of the moment. They rarely work. Be sure that you know ahead of time what you will do if you don't get the response you are looking for.

Exercise 21
Getting Ready to Raise Issues

The purpose of this exercise is to get some experience with the Raising Issues Worksheet. You will also be preparing for conversations you may wish to initiate after reading the next chapter.

- Prepare a master of the Raising Issues Worksheet and make several copies.

- Pick at least three real issues of current concern to you. Pick issues that, if resolved, would be of benefit to you and to the company.

- Do the preparation steps on all three issues.

- Find a co-worker whose opinion you respect and who can also keep conversations private. You don't want to review your preparation with someone who might then gossip about it with co-workers. Your Human Resources representative may be a good resource for this exercise.

- Review your work on all three issues with this co-worker. Ask him or her to help you identify more objective ways of describing the problem and listing impact statements that will help you be prepared to state a persuasive case. He or she also may be able to help you think of alternative or more workable requests to make.

- Read the next chapter before starting the conversation for real.

Raising Issues Worksheet

Problem: Describe the issue in terms of goals, roles, and/or procedures.

....

....

....

....

Impact: Describe ways in which the issue is affecting the job you do.

....

....

....

Requests: What do you want from the other person?

....

....

....

....

Benefits: How will solving this issue benefit everyone involved?

....

....

....

Chapter Nine

Managing the Conversation

The Raising Issues Worksheet we discussed in the last chapter is used as a brainstorming tool. But brainstorming can be a messy process. By the time you are finished, your worksheet can be a jumble of scribbled notes, abbreviations, and crossed-out words, making it difficult to read without studying it closely to decipher what's on the page. In this chapter, we will present another form, the Raising Issues Discussion Form, which is presented at the end of the chapter. This form was designed for organizing the work you do on the worksheet. It also provides you with legible, coherent notes to use, if needed, during your discussion about the issue. You will use your responses on the Raising Issues Discussion Form as a guide to follow when you are engaged in raising issues. We will also discuss how to manage emotions that may arise during the conversation.

Guidelines for Raising Issues

You may be wondering if you should refer to written notes during a conversation. Why not? You have put a lot of time into your preparation. You have thought about it, put documentation together, and had conversations with co-workers to prepare a convincing case. Where is it written that you have to memorize all this stuff before you go into a conversation? Written notes can make a big difference. If the issue you are raising is highly complicated, written notes can help you avoid confusion and ensure that you won't forget to make some of your more persuasive arguments. You may be approaching someone whose position or personality leaves you feeling a little bit

> There's **nothing wrong** with referring **to written notes** during a **conversation.**

nervous. Having notes will provide some degree of security. You will have at hand everything you need to make a convincing case, knowing that if you get flustered, you have something to refer back to.

The Raising Issues Discussion Form is designed to accomplish two goals. First, it provides notes for your use during the conversation. Second, it will help you structure the conversation. The steps discussed in this section offer you a method for structuring conversations intended to resolve conflicts, offer suggestions, make requests, or otherwise make things happen through conversations with people at work. The form is designed to help you remember the structure in the heat of the moment.

The Raising Issues Discussion Form will help you sort out your thoughts so that you can go into the conversation knowing what you want to say. It provides a road map to follow that will help you structure the conversation and keep the discussion on track. Some of the conversations you need to start may involve strong differences of opinion. Sometimes the issues being discussed are emotionally charged, resulting in defensiveness that can disrupt a conversation. Or you may be uncomfortable with conflict and have a history of getting lost in the middle of a conversation, in spite of all the preparation you put into the topic beforehand.

The following sequence of steps can help you bring structure to your conversations.

Steps for Structuring Conversations

- Ask for time.
- Make a brief opening statement.
- If the answer is yes, focus on the details of any agreements reached.
- If the answer is no, focus on your description of the issue and its impact to persuade the other person that the situation deserves attention and action.
- After establishing agreement that the issue deserves action, look for a win-win solution.
- End the conversation by restating your understanding of any agreements reached.
- If no agreement is reached, describe your next steps, if any.

We will look at each of these steps in detail. Once you have completed your work on the Raising Issues Discussion Form, you will be ready to go. Take a deep breath. Remind yourself that your intention is to have a conversation with a professional colleague about work. This is not personal. It helps to remember that the other person probably means well. He or she is doing what makes sense to him or her. Your job is to persuade the other person to see things in a different way and to consider doing something differently. Take heart and take action. Remind yourself that the solution to your problem may be just a conversation away.

Asking for Time

Raising issues and dealing with conflicts is hard for some people. By the time they prepare and get up the courage to act, they may be so anxious to get the conversation over with that they neglect to make sure that this is an appropriate time for the other person to talk. The last thing you want to do is launch into your description of a problem and make a request, only to discover that the other person is late for a meeting or otherwise distracted by things he or she has to do.

You should start with a request that goes something like this: "Al, I want to talk about something important. It may take a few minutes of your time. Is this a good time to talk?" Asking for time and letting the other person know that you want to discuss something of some importance will accomplish two objectives. First, you will find out if this is in fact a good time for the other person. If not, find a time that will work better for both of you.

You don't want to make your request and have the other person say something like, "Well, I just don't agree with you and I was just about to leave my office. Can we talk about this next week?" Now you have tipped your hand. You have made your request and received an initial negative response without having had any time to try to persuade the person to see things differently. And now he or she has several days to think about your request. He or she may reflect on your conversation and be even more set in his or her opinion and resistant to persuasion the next time the two of you talk.

Suppose you ask for time and the person says, "Well, to tell you the truth, I am on my way out the door. But tell me, what's the problem?" Do your best not to get into a detailed description of your issue at this time. Defer the conversation, but do so without sounding ominous about it. Say something like the following: "Al, it is nothing to be concerned about. I have an idea about a way to better coordinate the efforts of our two teams. I would prefer to wait until you have time to discuss it. Then we can get into the details. Next week will be just fine for me."

In asking for time to talk, make it clear that there is something important you want to talk about. By doing so, you are much more likely to get the other person's full attention, which is your second objective in asking for this time. The request gives him or her a chance to put other things aside for the moment and listen to what you have to say. Again, note the importance of your topic, but avoid making it sound overly serious. You do want to get the other person's full attention. You don't want to do this in a way that will make the other person feel like he or she may have done something wrong and needs to get defensive.

Making Your Opening Statement

You may have done a lot of homework getting ready for this conversation. Your opening statement is not the time to use it. Don't start with a five-minute monologue with an elaborate description of the issue, thirteen impact statements, your request, and a hard sell on benefits for agreeing with you. Start with a brief description of the issue and your request. The other person may agree with your request right away without you having to do a song and dance routine, showcasing your masterpiece of a persuasive argument.

Open the conversation with a statement of the issue and of your specific request in regard to the issue. You may have brainstormed several possible versions of this request. Open with the request that might result in your most preferred outcome. Out of personal discomfort, some people start out by asking for less than they really want. They may be uncertain about making their request, so they ask for far less than they want, in hopes of easing their own discomfort. Others soften their request, hoping to minimize resistance or the possibility that they might be seen as brash or pushy. But starting out asking for less than you want leaves you in an odd position if the other person easily agrees to your request. What do you do then? End the conversation, thinking that you might have gotten what you really wanted if only you had asked for it? Your only other option is to try to expand the conversation and ask for even more than the other person has already agreed to. This is a clumsy strategy at best. So start out by asking for what you want most of all. If you can think of lesser requests to make, save them for a fallback position should you find you need to negotiate for a little less than you started out asking for.

Ask for what you want—**you just might** get it.

In the previous chapter, we used the worksheet to get ready for a conversation with Al. On the discussion form, I might write the following version of an opening statement. "Every day you make scheduling and production decisions for your team that end up affecting how my team is able to get its job done. I would like to meet with you prior to your staff meetings so that I can offer my input and know more about what your team will be doing. Are you willing to do that?"

When the Answer Is Yes

If the other person agrees with you, good for you! You acted and you made something happen. Now focus on what the two of you are agreeing to do. You may have prepared a long list of impact statements. You may even be a little disappointed that you didn't get a chance to display the brilliance of your reasoning. But it is far better to spend time preparing and not need it than to not prepare and find yourself desperately wishing that you had.

Discuss in detail what each of you is agreeing to do. Before ending the conversation, restate, in your own words, what you understand the agreements to be. In the conversation with Al, you may consider several different ways for you to be able to consult Al before his team gets together to plan its day. After looking at various options, you reach an agreement that seems to work for both of you. Summarizing your agreement before you end the conversation is one way to make sure that you and Al understand your next steps in the same way. If you see the agreement a bit differently than Al does, he will then have a chance to clarify the situation by stating what he thought the agreement was.

> **Make sure** that the two of you have **been involved** in the same **conversation.**

Don't underestimate the importance of this step. Misunderstandings of conversations are a frequent source of breakdown in teamwork. People meet and discuss something. Each then leaves the meeting with his or her understanding of the conversation. Unfortunately, people all too often differ in their interpretation of what just happened in the meeting. Such misunderstandings may involve vitally important details. Later, when teamwork between the two begins to break down, each of them begins to doubt the trustworthiness of the other person: "Look what she is doing. We talked about this and now she is doing the exact opposite of what we agreed to do. So much for honoring agreements. The only thing she cares about is her agenda."

I have seen this many times in consulting projects. A person may be operating on his or her interpretation of an agreement reached with a co-worker. But differing interpretations lead to differing expectations and actions. On the basis of their own interpretation, others on the team judge the person harshly, since it looks to them as if he or she is failing to honor the agreement. Invariably in such situations, when I have a chance to speak to people privately about what is going on, I am given two very different descriptions of the same agreement. Each of them was operating in good faith on what he or she thought the other party had agreed to. Had one person taken the trouble to end the original meeting with a summary of the agreement, as he or she understood it at the time, the co-workers could have avoided a breakdown in teamwork and all the subsequent personalized assumptions about each other's trustworthiness and reliability.

When the Answer Is No

So what do you do when you make a request and get a no or a noncommittal response? Do you fold up your tent and go home? Absolutely not. Now is the time to draw on your preparation. In dealing with a no, you have to direct the conversation so that you can discover the answers to two questions:

- Does the other person agree that a problem exists?
- If the other person agrees that a problem does exist and the answer is still no, does he or she object to something about the specific request you are making or the solution you are proposing?

A no is often just the beginning of a **great problem-solving** conversation.

Discovering the answers to these two questions determines your strategy throughout the rest of the conversation. Begin with the first question, determining whether the other person agrees that a problem exists that deserves attention. Let's go back to our conversation with Al. Suppose you have put the question to him, asking for the opportunity to consult with him before he makes decisions about schedules and resource allocation for his team. Al pauses for a moment and, being a man of few words, says, "Nah, I'd rather leave things the way they are."

Maybe Al is declining your request because he simply doesn't think there is a problem. Asking for the opportunity to consult him daily is no small matter and can easily be seen by him as an unnecessary inconvenience. This is especially true if he doesn't see that the way he is doing things is causing a problem.

Support for Your Arguments

Now the time you spent preparing for this conversation will pay off. You need to focus on persuading Al that, in fact, the current situation is having a serious impact on the company. You must present an argument so compelling that Al will come to agree that, indeed, this situation deserves attention and action.

This is where the rest of the information on your worksheet, described in the following sections, will be useful. Keep exploring the impact of the situation. Ask questions to discover how the other person sees the situation. Remember, the other person is unlikely to consent to doing anything any differently until he or she is persuaded that, in fact, your concerns need to be taken seriously.

Description of the Issue

The first step in supporting your argument is to describe the situation, emphasizing the impact the current decision-making process is having on your team. When you complete this section of the form, you will need to go back to your Raising Issues Worksheet. List the ways in which the issue can be described, in terms of goals, roles, procedures, and decision making. You might be able to describe the same issue in several ways. List these descriptions, starting with the clearest, most accurate, and most easily communicated.

In your conversation, start with your most convincing argument. You might say something like this:

> *Every morning you meet with your team and make scheduling decisions. Sometimes this changes the flow of the work from the previous day, but our team can be unaware of the change until almost noon. When we finally figure out what is going on, we are already hopelessly behind. Just yesterday we had to work two hours overtime to catch up. Do you see how our lack of information is creating a problem that is raising costs for our division?*

Note the last question. Don't be afraid to directly ask if the other person understands the problem. What you are trying to do is draw the other person out. You want him or her to elaborate on how he or she sees the situation. You want to see if he or she understands the situation and its impact in the same way that you do. This will help you come up with more persuasive arguments by adding information that will help the other person understand why you are concerned about this issue.

Impact Statements

Take special care with this section of your Raising Issues Discussion Form—you may end up referring to it several times during the conversation. Prioritize your list of impact statements in terms of their power to persuade the other person that your issue deserves serious consideration.

Suppose Al says, "We post the scheduling information on the company intranet. That ought to be enough to give you what you need."

This provides you with more information. Maybe you didn't know the information was posted, and maybe this will solve the problem. But, for the sake of this example, let's imagine that the information isn't posted quickly enough to do you any good. You might respond like this:

Yes, the information is posted where we can find it. Unfortunately, your staff meeting is at the start of the day and decisions made at that meeting make an immediate difference in the workflow from your team to mine. Unfortunately, the intranet posting sometimes isn't completed until almost noon. By the time we get your schedule, we have to scramble to catch up. If I could meet with you just before your meeting, I would be able to find out what you have in mind for your team that day and offer you information about how that might affect my department. Are you willing to give this a try?

> **Never expect** someone to grant a **request that fails** to take his or her **needs into account.**

If this doesn't work, try an impact statement that appeals directly to the self-interest of the other person, such as this:

Just yesterday our boss sent me an email telling me that she wants to talk about overtime in my department. This coordination problem is the source of most of our overtime. If we can't solve this problem, Al, I think we are both going to end up looking bad. She will have every reason to wonder why you and I can't do a better job of coordinating the workflow between our two teams. Don't you agree that we should find a solution to this problem before she feels she has to intervene?

Benefits

On your discussion form, you should brainstorm and list benefits to be derived from solving the problem. Be sure to include any benefits that might directly appeal to the interests of the person you are about to approach.

Use your statements at this point in the discussion. You might say something like this:

> *Al, if we are able to solve this problem, you and I can take credit for reducing our division's overtime costs. We will also be able to assure our boss that we are living up to our corporate value of solving problems at the level of the team without upper management having to intervene. It will reduce the stress between our two departments and make us both look good. What do you think? Are you willing to give this a try?*

I could probably go on with many more examples, but I hope you understand the strategy that should guide you at this point in a difficult conversation. If the other person doesn't agree that a problem exists, your job is to provide the information to convince him or her that this situation demands resolution.

Agreements

After establishing agreement that the issue deserves action, look for a win-win solution. You will have reached a turning point in the conversation once the other person finally agrees that the situation deserves attention and action. Now you are both on the same side of the issue. Both of you now agree that something needs to be done. The next step is to find a solution that meets the needs of everyone involved.

Looking for a Win-Win Solution

Your principal objective in the discussion up to now has been persuasion. Once the other person agrees that some solution needs to be found, your stance should shift from persuasion to flexibility. By now, you may have learned a great deal about the other person's view of the issue. You may discover that their resistance to your request does not stem from their failure to see that the issue is serious. They may have seen the impact of the problem all along. What they may actually be objecting to is your particular solution. You may have made a request that they don't see how they can grant without seriously compromising the work they have to do.

For example, Al may finally say something like the following:

I can see that this is a problem, but I just don't think it is practical for me to meet with you every day before my team meeting. We start the day with that meeting. We can't get production started for the day until we get together to review the inventory and the outstanding orders. My team can't just sit around until you and I finish our meeting. I just don't think that is practical.

This is what so often happens in working things out with co-workers. Each of us has our own set of concerns and obligations to meet. Any change requested by one person must be filtered through the interests and needs of the other person involved. This is why you must look for a win-win solution in any problem-solving conversation—that is, a solution that turns out to be a win for both people involved.

There are many ways to get there **from here...** unless, of course, you **just want** to be right.

That is why flexibility is so important. You may start out with a very specific view of an issue and its possible resolution. But the conversation may reveal a broader picture of the issue and how any solution might affect the other person. You may not get the exact solution you requested. If you do arrive at an agreement that solves the problem, it may not look exactly like what you wanted, but you still will have accomplished your goal.

For example, there are a variety of possible outcomes in our conversation with Al. You and Al might agree to meet immediately after his staff meeting every morning. The two of you might decide that a telephone call would do. Or you might work together on an information sheet that Al will fill out during his meetings that will include all the data you need to organize the work of your team. Another solution might be to have someone on Al's staff enter the data on the intranet in real time. This will make the information available online as the decisions are being made.

Flexibility in looking for a mutually acceptable solution is critically important. Some people get so fixated on one solution that they are unable to see that any number of other agreements might also meet their needs. You don't want these conversations to be about "winning." If you consistently insist on things going exactly your way, you will inevitably alienate the very people you need to be able to work with effectively.

Recording Your Understanding of Agreements Reached

To ensure that you both understand agreements in the same way, summarize the agreements before ending the conversation. Use this space on your discussion form during the conversation. You will hopefully be reaching some agreements with the other person. As you do so, write them down. You will be ending the conversation with a summary, in your own words, of agreements reached during the conversation. Notes taken during the conversation can help ensure that both you and the other person leave the conversation with the same understanding of any agreements the two of you have reached.

As we discussed earlier, this can help you avoid any crucial misunderstandings. Even in the most collaborative and cordial of relationships, people sometimes hear what they want to hear. Summarizing one final time gives each of you the chance to recognize and resolve any misunderstandings that might lead to later problems.

There are other reasons why an ending summary can be so useful. People get distracted in conversations. They may have a lot of work to do and be thinking about something else, nodding their head in agreement to something that was said without fully realizing what they just consented to do. Misunderstandings can also be the result of two people using the same words but understanding them in different ways. Again, an ending summary is one last effort to uncover any ambiguities in your agreements that might lead to later problems.

When No Agreement Is Reached

Failure to reach any agreement at all is a difficult moment for any of us. You want to deal with these moments carefully. By the end of a conversation that produced no acceptable outcome, you may be frustrated and bewildered by the other person's unwillingness to comprehend the brilliance of your carefully stated case. But your frustration must be put aside. You are talking to a co-worker, and you need to deal with this moment in a way that will not do damage to your relationship with him or her.

If no agreement is reached during the conversation, you may decide to simply thank the other person for his or her time and move on, knowing that you win some and you lose some. Such is the nature of life in an organization.

Another option is to end the conversation by telling the other person that you intend to keep this issue on the table for discussion. For example, you could say, "I understand that this situation just doesn't look that serious to you right now. For now we will do nothing any differently. I do want you to know that I will continue to monitor this situation. I will be coming back to you if further problems arise to keep you posted on the ongoing impact of the problem."

On the other hand, you may have decided before going into the conversation that the problem is so serious that it must be addressed, whether or not the person you are approaching agrees with you. If this is the case, think very carefully about how you will handle this moment gracefully and honestly. The last thing you want to do is go to some higher authority without telling the other person you are going to do this. That is a trustbuster for sure. So you want to be honest about your intentions—but in a way that will avoid alienating the other person.

For example, Al, in spite of all your persuasion, might still not see the issue as a problem. You might say something like this:

Al, I had really hoped that you and I could find a solution to this problem that would meet both of our needs. I just cannot continue to justify the overtime this situation is causing my team, and our boss is beginning to wonder what is going on. I am going to have to review this situation with her in a meeting tomorrow. I want to make sure that your opinion is fairly represented. Are you willing to go to that meeting with me so that you can represent your own point of view?

Managing the Emotions of Conflict

Conflict is inevitable. It can also be dangerous to your relationships and your career. Learning to cope with the emotional experience of conflict is one of your most important career success skills. For some, whose emotions tend to spiral out of control, learning to deal with conflict professionally can be a career survival skill. Let's take a look at the life cycle of conflict and explore ways to avoid some of the emotional land mines that can cause serious damage.

When Something Happens
That Triggers an Emotional Response

This is the most dangerous time for many of us. Someone does something—or fails to do something—that violates your expectations. The response, for some of us, is immediate and highly charged. I once had an experience of anger on the job that I can look back on now as an important learning point for me. One of my co-workers did something that I felt was completely unacceptable. What he did, I thought at the time, was a violation of ethical and professional standards. My response was immediate and highly emotional. I can even remember the physical expression of my anger. I could feel my chest constricting. My breathing became strained. My heart rate increased. I knew that my temper was about to get out of control and there wasn't a thing I could do about it.

I exploded in a fit of righteous anger. In the heat of my emotional overload, I was completely undisciplined in how I expressed myself. My mind was filled with judgments and accusations and I expressed them freely. In due time, my emotions began to ebb, and I started to think and communicate more rationally. As my anger subsided, I became embarrassed by how inappropriately I had expressed myself.

There I stood, the expert on how to not take things personally. Where was the deep breath? What happened to remembering to professionalize rather than personalize? Where was the guy who stands in front of groups talking about the dangers of conflict and letting unbridled emotions run freely? I would have been deeply shamed for a client or one of the groups I have trained to see me in that moment. I had become my own case study on how *not* to express oneself at work.

As the other person and I talked, I realized that he had a perfectly good reason for making the decision he had made. We still disagreed about the choice he had made. I would have had him make a different choice. But it was one of those issues over which people with good intentions can find themselves in disagreement. I had known the other person for some time. He was anything but a jerk. He was driven by his own sense

When people disagree with you, it **may not** mean they don't **understand** you. They **may just disagree.**

of ethics and integrity. I knew that he was the last person who would intentionally do anything self-serving at the expense of his professional standards. He and I just saw the situation differently. All the emotion I brought into the conversation had sidetracked us, for the moment, from having a productive conversation. And some of the things I said were clearly inappropriate and potentially damaging to our relationship. Fortunately, as we exchanged views, we were able to patch up any damage

I had done. But no relationship can stand up to very many of these kinds of outbursts. Sooner or later, the person on the receiving end will begin to lose his or her willingness to forgive.

This experience was an important reminder. Conflict, particularly when the issue involves something we feel strongly about, can be dangerous ground to tread. For me, and perhaps for you as well, the most appropriate response when something happens is *no* response at all—at least until I am able to get my emotions under control. Almost every time I have acted in the heat of anger, I have said things I quickly regretted.

The preparation steps we talked about in the previous chapter provide a refuge. The structure of the Raising Issues Worksheet forces us to think more objectively. If something happens that triggers a strong response, defer the conversation, if at all possible, before you shoot yourself in the foot. Even five minutes with the worksheet might be all you need to phrase a response that is more likely to make a positive difference and less likely to do damage to your credibility.

Gossip is poisonous— talk to the person **who needs** to hear about **your concern** or **don't talk about** it at all.

The Time Between the Event and the Conversation

The time between the event that triggers the need for a conversation and the conversation itself can be used very well. You can use the Raising Issues Worksheet to prepare for a conversation that will make something happen.

Or you can use the time to nurse your resentment and anger. Sometimes people hold onto a resentment and constantly mull it over in their mind. It's a bit like a dog chewing a bone. Rather than getting ready for a conversation, we might use the time to build an even stronger case for what a jerk the other person is or how unfairly we are being treated.

When entire groups start doing this, some real damage can occur. Teammates might spend time complaining about some situation behind closed doors. The more the group talks about it, the more real and unquestioned the "wrong" becomes. Since "everyone" seems to agree with us, our anger and resentment take an even deeper hold on us, making it all the more difficult for anyone on the team to see the issue clearly or act to change it professionally.

Sometimes I work with teams in creating interpersonal norms or cultural guiding principles. I always recommend that these teams consider not talking to anyone about a problem unless it is the person who can do something about it and not indulging in gossip and complaining as part of the team's core values.

Use your time well. If something is of concern to you, get out a Raising Issues Worksheet and go to work on it. Then talk about it—with the one person who can actually do something about it.

Raising the Issue and Making Your Request

If you are upset about an issue you are about to raise, do everything you can to leave your feelings out of the conversation. Emotions disrupt your ability to speak clearly. They also make it difficult for the other person to hear you out nondefensively. Prepare your opening statement carefully. Run it by a co-worker to make sure you have taken all the emotion and personalizing out of your phrasing of the issue.

After nearly twenty years of teaching this skill, I had a recent experience of making a poorly phrased opening statement in a role-play demonstration in front of a group. The issue the group and I had chosen for the demonstration was that of a team member failing to keep some of the agreements the team had created about how to participate in team meetings. I opened with, "Jim, apparently you don't like to keep our team's agreements about how to put issues on the agenda for team meetings. I would like you to submit your items in advance so that I can do a better job of planning the meeting."

The volunteer who was my partner was very good at role-play. He responded, "What do you mean I don't like to keep our team agreements? I participate on this team and keep agreements just like everyone else." What I was trying to demonstrate for the group was how to raise issues appropriately. Instead, my opener included my accusation that Jim didn't like to keep the team agreements. That is a personalized description of the issue.

This is how I *should* have phrased my opener: "Jim, I noticed that you added a couple of significant discussion items to the agenda after the meeting started. Would you please submit them to me before the meeting so that I can do a better job of planning the meeting?" Note how the second phrasing, which I thought of too late for it to make a difference, described only the need to stick to a procedure. This would have been a much more effective way to begin.

Prepare carefully. If possible, enlist the aid of someone who can help you polish your opening statement.

When the Other Person Doesn't Agree with You

It is very easy to react emotionally when you describe a problem that concerns you and the other person just doesn't agree with you. He or she may not agree that the problem is having a serious enough impact to be taken seriously. Or he or she may not agree to grant your request. Early in my career, I co-facilitated with Bob Solum, my late friend and business partner who was one of the coauthors of my first book, *The Mission-Driven Organization,* quite a few workshops on stress management. Bob used to point out that life is filled with moments when we are tested in our ability to cope with stress. When something stressful would happen, he would say, "Hey, Bob. It's just another pop quiz from the Universe."

Conversations to resolve conflict are just that—pop quizzes. We find ourselves being tested in our ability to keep the conversation squarely in the professional arena where it belongs. When people don't agree with us, the natural tendency is to assume that they just don't understand what we are saying. If they understood us, they would, of course, agree with us. The longer the conversation goes on without the other person agreeing with us, the easier it is for us to grow impatient. We begin to have thoughts like, "What is wrong with this person? It should be perfectly obvious that my plan makes perfect sense. He is just driven by his own agenda. If it isn't his idea, it is not a good idea." The more we indulge in thoughts like this, the more likely we are to end up saying something we will later regret.

When in a conversation that is not going as we had planned, we need to keep reminding ourselves not to take things so personally. We need to remember that, indeed, sometimes people do not see things the way we do. The world does not and will not revolve around our personal needs and perspectives. We need to continue to trust in the intentions of the other person and remind ourselves of our commitment to communicate professionally. We also need to accept the fact that we will not always get everything we want. This is a fact of life for all of us as mem-

> **It takes discipline** to know when **to quit** explaining **your point** of view and **accept** that you gave it **your best shot.**

Exercise 22
Taking Action

- In exercise 21, "Getting Ready to Raise Issues," you completed worksheets on three issues. Choose the one that is least likely to result in an emotional confrontation. If all of the issues you prepared seem like risky ones to raise, choose another issue. You want your first experience with raising issues to be successful. The issue you raise doesn't have to involve addressing a huge conflict. You may have a suggestion you want to make to your boss or a minor problem in teamwork to work out with a co-worker.

- If necessary, follow the preparation steps with a Raising Issues Worksheet. Then organize your information on the Raising Issues Discussion Form.

- Now act!

- Afterward, review the conversation in your mind. Evaluate how thoroughly prepared you were for the conversation. Did you follow the steps as described in this chapter? If the conversation got off track, where did you deviate from the steps? What could you do to improve your success in raising issues the next time out?

- Choose another issue. Prepare and act again.

- If a conversation doesn't go according to plan, don't be hard on yourself. Congratulate yourself for having the courage to act. Learn what you can from each conversation so that you can continue to improve your skills.

bers of organizations. In the end, the quality of our life and career will be determined more by how we accept moments like this than by the number of arguments we have won.

Exercise 22 will help you start making the work you have put into this book pay off by improving teamwork through conversation.

Raising Issues Discussion Form

Remember to ask for time.

Opening Statement: Formulate a briefly stated request.

....

....

If the answer is yes, clarify your understanding of any agreements reached and list them in the "Agreements" section below. If the answer is no, does the other person agree that the situation deserves attention and action?

Support for Your Argument

Descriptions of the Issue: List ways of describing the issue, emphasizing teamwork.

....

....

Impact Statements: Make a prioritized listing of impacts on the job.

....

....

Benefits: List benefits the other person will attain if he or she agrees with your request.

....

....

Agreements: Look for solutions that meet both parties' needs. Record your understanding of agreements reached. To ensure that you both understand the agreements in the same way, summarize the agreements before ending the conversation.

....

....

....

Part Three

Making the Good Relationships Even Better

Chapter Ten

Living up to Your Aspirations

Like most people, you have a lot to do. It is so easy to become caught up in the busyness of life that we forget to ask ourselves where we are going. Not long ago I took a day hike in the mountains. It was a gorgeous Northwest summer day and a great day to get away from the city. I set out on a trail that led to an overlook I'd visited once before, and I was looking forward to sipping tea and taking in the view.

The trail was much steeper than I had remembered. After a while, the hike turned into hard work. My thigh muscles were burning and sweat was pouring into my eyes. I found myself huffing and puffing, wondering when I was ever going to get to the top. The trail was quite narrow with a long fall to my right if I were to lose my balance, so I had to keep my eyes on the path to make sure I didn't lose my footing.

After a while I realized what I was doing. I had turned the hike into work, a task to get behind me. I had forgotten that I was there to enjoy myself. I was spending so much time making sure I didn't fall off the cliff and whining about my sore legs that it hadn't occurred to me to pause, catch my breath, and take a look at the scenery. By doing so, I found that I could enjoy myself and remember that my purpose wasn't just to get to the top. My purpose was to have a relaxing day amidst the beauty of the mountains.

Our work lives are often like this. We get so caught up in the demands and details of the work each day that we forget to ask ourselves where we are going and what we can do to find more satisfaction in the journey of life itself. Little wonder that midlife crises always include the struggle to find meaning in our lives and our work. We come

> **Sometimes** we can become so **caught up** in the **details** of the work that **we forget why** we are working in the **first place.**

to the realization that the years have been quickly slipping by while we have been so focused on getting up the trail without falling off. After a while, it is no longer enough just to work. It is no longer enough to demonstrate our capabilities. We want the hard work and hours we devote to our work to add to the significance and meaning in our lives.

Without meaning, we ultimately feel empty. We begin to think that maybe we took a wrong turn somewhere on the trail. At that point we jump to the conclusion that maybe what we need is a new trail. A new path, we are sure, is where we will find that missing something our hearts are yearning for. So people change careers or wish they could, all the while thinking that the perfect path is out there somewhere. But it certainly can't be the path they are already on.

Setting Your Steering Point

One of the absolute requirements for a full and satisfying life is living life as an expression of personal vision. This includes creating clarity about your destination. Where are you going? Why are you going there? And how can you make the journey itself as important as the destination? If you are going to work so hard to stay on the path, it is essential to have a purpose in mind to help you make choices at various decision points on the trail.

Years ago, I led a retreat for an event that was taking place outside of Seattle. The journey required a trip across the waters of Puget Sound. One of the executives had a boat and sailed a group of us to the resort. Being from the Midwest, I had never been aboard a sailboat and was excited to give this a try. It was a calm day, however, and we needed to use the motor part of the way. Our host asked me if I wanted to take the helm. Then he pointed to a cluster of trees on the horizon. "That's your steering point. Just keep the bow aimed at those trees, and we'll end up where we want to go."

Our lives are like that. We need a steering point, a destination on the horizon that helps us make steering corrections along the way. Lacking a steering point, we will likely one day wonder, "Is this all there is?"

But our vision for our lives needs to include more that just a desired outcome. It needs to also include guidelines for enjoying the journey of life itself, living it one day at a time and living it fully. Someone once made a comment about one of the differences between the Western and Eastern approaches to life. People from our culture are reared to be goal oriented. Everything is focused on reaching an objective, completing a task, or managing to arrive at some particular state in life when at last we believe we will be content. Eastern philosophies lead people to pay more attention to the process than to the outcome. That is one reason you see so much attention to detail in Japanese art and handicrafts. The artisan isn't in such a hurry to get finished and move on to the next thing. Total involvement with each step of the process leads to more satisfaction with the process itself. It can also lead to highly desirable outcomes.

I recently spent some time with a young professional in one of my consulting projects. At twenty-eight, he was unhappy because he wasn't in a management position that carried a lofty title and more responsibility. I remembered my own impatience to "get there" when I was his age. I wanted to smile and assure him that he was already "there," that life was in all likelihood bringing him the experiences he needed to get ready for the next step in his development. But I knew that this would probably make little sense to him.

I used to think that reaching contentment with the journey of life was something that could come only with age and experience. I feel differently about that now. Contentment was just as available to me in my twenties and thirties as it is now. But I was in such a hurry to get somewhere—although just where I wanted to go was something I wasn't very clear about—that I wasn't enjoying the journey. I didn't even know what I was looking for. I just felt certain that there was some proper alignment of life's circumstances that was necessary for my happiness. Until I got there, I felt all I could do was grind my teeth with impatience to get on with it.

Sadly, I know that I completely missed the opportunity to take a deep breath, exhale, and enjoy the fullness of life each day. Don't waste any more time waiting for life to turn out. It already has. It is right there in front of you.

You will need to do the following exercise in a journal or at your computer. I encourage you to engage with this exercise fully. I know from personal experience and from working with clients that this one piece of work can make a big difference in the quality of your life. Unless we take time now and then to reestablish our steering point, life has a way of happening to us. Then one day we may wake up and wonder where the years went and how we wound up where we are. The following exercise is a significant step toward living a life of purpose and meaning.

Exercise 23
Five Years from Now

- Imagine that a journalist is visiting your company five years from now. She meets you and is so struck by the person you are that she decides to write an article about you. Write that article as if it were written by someone else who is a real fan of yours.

- As you write this article, don't hold anything back. You don't have to show it to anyone. When I have done this exercise, I have written such a glowing description of the kind of person I want to be that I would be embarrassed to let anyone else read it. If I knew someone were going to see it, I would soften some of the things I write about my deepest hopes for myself and the person I want to be.

- In writing this article, start with how you want your working life to be five years from now. You may be hoping that by then you will have broken out into a new career or have a job at a different company. You may write about that if you wish, but in doing so you run the risk of adding even more fuel to the fires of any discontentment you may be feeling in your current work. Besides, the purpose of the exercise is to generate maximum satisfaction in the job you have now, even if you are making plans to move on someday. So for now, focus on the job you have currently. When you are finished, you may want to work on an alternative scenario, writing the article as if you have successfully made a career or job transition you may have been thinking about.

- Here are some factors to consider in writing your article:

Professional success. What would you like to be doing in your company in five years? Write about the work you see yourself doing and what you will have achieved professionally by that time.

Your relationships at work. How do you want others to perceive you? What do you want them to admire about your contributions as a team member? What would you like them to appreciate about the personal contributions you make to their lives?

Family life. Don't restrict yourself to your professional life. What do you want your personal life to look five years from now? Is a relationship in the picture? Marriage? Improvements in the one you're in now? Children? What do you see happening in this aspect of your personal life? How do you want it to look? How are the people involved contributing to the quality of each other's lives?

Your health. How do you envision your health and self-care? What will you have done to achieve that level of wellness over the next five years? How will this contribute to the quality of your living?

Spiritual life and personal development. What do you see yourself doing to develop your spiritual connection, however you might define that? What impact will that have on the quality of your being? Will you be making more time for other forms of personal development? How will that affect you over the next five years?

Friendships. What will your social life look like in five years? Where will you be making friends, during working hours and beyond? What is the quality of these relationships? In what ways do these relationships add meaning and intimacy to your life and to theirs?

Recreational activities. Are there things you have always wanted to do but have never done? Imagine you were to start now. What impact would that be having on you in five years?

(continued)

Community service. What do you see yourself doing in five years that in some way makes a contribution to society at large? What would you like to be doing then? How would that contribute to others and how would it affect you personally?

- Include quotes. The journalist is able to interview people in both your personal and professional life. Include direct quotes from co-workers, customers, family members, friends, and anyone else who represents a significant factor in your article. What would you want these people to say about you if you could be exactly the kind of person your heart is directing you to be? This is no time for false modesty. You are describing your ideal self. Make sure your quotes reflect the quality of the professional you intend to be as well as the love and humanity you offer to people lucky enough to know you.

- Think carefully about the kind of person you want to be. No matter what aspect of your life you are writing about in the article, develop a clear picture of the personal qualities you want to bring to your life and to the lives of those you encounter. This can range from brief contacts with people on the job and enduring relationships at work to friends and your most intimate relationships.

Asking for Feedback

Earlier in the book, we talked about how we never quite see ourselves the way others see us. Your work in the previous exercise will have established a clear picture of the kind of life you want to have and the kind of person you want to be, personally and professionally. Realizing your vision means taking an honest look at the person you are today and looking for two things. The first thing to ask is, Where are you already on track? Then begin developing those personal qualities that will take you in the right direction, given your steering point. The second thing to ask is, How are you currently not quite the person you would like to be? In what areas do you need to take a close look at yourself and set about making some significant improvements?

Some of the things you will need to do will be obvious. For example, you may see yourself rising to a certain position or entering into a particular job that requires specific skills. If you don't have the necessary training or experience to get there, it is obvious what you need to do, starting now, to achieve your personal goals. Create a plan to start developing yourself as needed.

However, there is one aspect of personal development that isn't as easily accomplished. It involves seeing some of our personal flaws. These flaws may be glaringly obvious to others, but we simply don't see them. So we cruise along in life blissfully unaware that there are adjustments we could make in our approaches to others that would make a huge difference in the relationships that are so important to our professional success and personal fulfillment. But without a chance to look in a mirror, we may never realize there is a wart right there on the end of our nose. It's in plain sight of everyone but us.

The purpose of this section is to provide a structure to follow in asking your manager, team members, and peers for feedback that will help you discover blind spots in your perception of yourself. Increasing your self-awareness is one of the most important ingredients in developing a personal development action plan.

Preparing for the Conversation

I am going to ask you to seek out two or three people and ask them for feedback. Doing this could turn out to be one of the most valuable things you do outside of reading this book. If you choose the right people to ask and listen carefully to what they have to say, you may be surprised at what you discover about aspects of yourself that you have never seen clearly. Read the instructions carefully. Choose the right people to ask, and phrase your questions following the suggestions I'll give you. Listen to what these people say to you. Then act on what you learn. You could very well discover the one or two most important things you need to do if you are to realize your vision.

Who to Ask

Choose two or three people who are likely to be willing to speak frankly with you. Try to find people who are good observers and whose opinions you can trust. You should also seek out at least one person you think may have issues with you. You may learn something very useful about yourself, and your willingness to ask this person to give you feedback may help ease things between you. Also seek out one or two peers if you have some who are in a good position to share perspectives with you.

Identifying Areas for Questions

You will find a number of questions to ask in exercise 24. Nevertheless, make certain you are prepared to ask questions that will meet your needs. Review the work you did in exercise 23, Five Years from Now.

Be sure to phrase questions to discover how others see you with respect to some of the most important personal qualities you want to develop.

How to Behave During the Conversation

Most people are uncomfortable with feedback, whether they are giving it or receiving it. You are asking people to have a conversation with you that can provide you with valuable information. This is a conversation that the other person may find to be uncomfortable, especially if you happen to be that person's manager. Your reaction to his or her feedback will have a lot to do with how open and detailed the other person will be in talking to you. Here are some things to remember:

- *Schedule this conversation at a comfortable time in a comfortable place.* Make sure that the other person has ample time and is not distracted by something else that needs to be done soon. Choose a setting that is comfortable for the other person. For example, if this person works for you, do not use your office. You have too many symbols of authority there. Go to the other person's office or, better yet, meet in a casual place, such as a coffee shop away from work.
- *Remind yourself to be relaxed and casual.* This conversation may in fact make you very nervous. Don't let it show. If you do, it may make the other person less willing to speak up honestly.
- *Listen.* You are asking for information. Listen to what the other person is saying. Stay focused on the other person, not on your internal commentary on what you are hearing. To make sure you understand, paraphrase what you are hearing. Stating in your own words what you think the other person is saying is a great way to clarify any distortions in your own listening. Make certain that you fully understand the feedback and do not leave with any misunderstandings.
- *Ask open-ended questions that require a detailed response.* The questions in exercise 24 have been carefully phrased to elicit information. For example, don't ask, "Is there anything I do that makes me difficult to disagree with?" If the other person is uncomfortable with this question, it would be very easy for him or her to evade the topic by saying, "No, not at all." Consequently, I have phrased all the questions in a way that leaves less "wiggle room" and is more likely to generate useful information. Phrase questions like this: "What are two or three things I do that may at times make me

difficult to disagree with?" Before writing your own questions to supplement those found in exercise 24, be sure to study how I have phrased the sample questions and phrase your own in a similar way.

- *Do not defend yourself.* If you start offering excuses or examples that contradict the people you talk with, they are likely to shut down and stop offering information. They didn't agree to this conversation to get into an argument with you. You have asked them to share their perception of you. Give them the courtesy of listening. Remind yourself that even if you disagree with their perception, it is still their perception. When you hear something that is surprising or that is not consistent with your own perception of yourself, remind yourself that you are probably doing—or not doing—something that contributes to the other person's perception of you. Find out as much as you can so that you can begin to behave in a way that will have people see you the way you want to be seen.

- *Ask for examples to clarify broad generalizations.* If the other person uses words that are open to interpretation, ask for more specific information. If, for example, the other person says something like, "At times you are rude," or "I wish you weren't so hard to talk to," ask for more specific information to clarify what they mean. Ask follow-up questions such as, "I really want to understand what you are saying. Is there something I do or fail to do that gives you that impression? Is it my tone of voice? Is it an expression on my face that I might not be aware of? Is there something I say that leaves you with this feeling about me?"

- *Take action.* If feedback is accurate and apologies are in order, apologize. See if the two of you can reach an agreement on how to handle similar situations in the future.

You may wish to think about what has been said. You are under no obligation to respond to everything that has been said immediately. Tell the person that you appreciate his or her willingness to talk to you and that he or she has given you a lot to think about. If a follow-up conversation is appropriate, promise to get back to the person. Then make sure that you do just that.

Even if some of the feedback seems off the mark, don't get defensive. You can always say something like this:

You have described me in some ways that surprise me. They don't fit my concept of myself at all. But I promise you that I will think about what you have said and observe myself more closely in the future. I would appreciate it if you would call this to my attention if you see me doing the same thing in the future. Most of us have things we do out of habit, and I may be doing this without any awareness of how it affects people around me. You may be able to help me see it more clearly.

A Suggested Structure for the Conversation

In this section we will discuss a structure that can be used for the conversation.

Establishing Your Purpose

First state that you have asked for time because you want to ask for some feedback on how you are doing in your job as a leader (or fellow manager or team member). Point out that most of us have things about ourselves that we don't see clearly and that you want the benefit of the person's perception, especially regarding things you can do to improve.

Putting the Other Person at Ease

Point out that you are aware that this kind of conversation doesn't happen very often. This is especially true when you are talking to someone who reports to you. Most feedback goes the other way—from you to them. Assure the person that you want him or her to be open with you, that you very much want to hear what he or she has to say.

Self-disclosure can be disarming, but only if it is genuine. For example, if you are yourself uncomfortable about this conversation, say so. "I don't know about you, but conversations like this make me uneasy because I'm not quite sure what I am going to hear. Nevertheless, I promise to do my best to relax and listen." Imagine how you might feel if your own boss asked you for feedback, and talk about that: "I was thinking about how I would feel if my boss asked me for feedback. I realized that you might feel a little uneasy about me asking you these kinds of questions."

Exploring Areas of Interest to You

Now it is time to proceed to ask questions, exploring some of the topics in the following exercise. Add your own questions to make certain that you get at information vital to you. Be sure to take notes so you don't lose any valuable information.

Exercise 24
Asking the Right Questions

Leadership

- What are the two or three things I do best as a leader?

- What are two things I should do more often that would make me a better manager/team member?

- What are two things I should do less often that would make me a better manager/team member?

Team Development

- How can I do a better job of leading (or participating on) this team (department, company, etc.)?

- What should I be doing more of to share my vision and goals for our team?

- How can I do a better job of getting people involved in setting those goals?

- What could I be doing to better represent the needs of this team to upper management?

Participation/Decision Making

- In what areas do you need more authority for making decisions?

- How can I make myself more available for your input on decisions I have to make?

- What could I be doing to better share my own thinking about decisions I make?

- What are some examples of times when I am slow to make decisions?

- How about instances when I make decisions too quickly or without giving enough consideration to how it affects people on this team?

Coaching

- In what ways do I need to pay more attention to the performance of people on this team?

- How can I improve in my response to good performance?

- How can I improve in my response to poor performance?

- Describe examples of poor performance that is not getting an appropriate response from me.

Conflict

- In what ways do I need to do a better job of dealing with conflict on this team?

- What are some ways in which I might discourage people from expressing disagreements with me that really should be discussed?

- What do I do that might be overly harsh or overly soft in dealing with conflict?

Cultural Development

- What do you like most about working on this team?

- What do you like least about working on this team?

- What needs to happen to make this a better place to work?

Interpersonal Qualities

- Most people have qualities that people talk about with each other but not with the person him- or herself. When people talk about me, what complaints seem to come up from time to time?

- Is there any one thing you would like to see me do that would make me easier to work for and make this a better place for you to work?

Closing the Conversation

At the end of the conversation, thank the person for being willing to talk openly with you and assure him or her that you will carefully consider what he or she had to say. Let the person know that you are open to this kind of feedback at any time and look forward to addressing areas you are learning about.

Personal Development

Vision without action is little better than daydreaming. Asking for feedback and then doing nothing with it will be a waste of your time and others'. So we'll close the loop with action planning.

The following exercise is not meant to be a comprehensive plan based on every chapter of this book. Previous exercises have suggested things for you to do, many of which you may have done by now. The following action steps are focused on identifying things you need to start doing to work toward making your steering point a reality. You will also be doing some work to address any personal development needs that surfaced when you asked people for feedback. You may wish to return to your action plan after reading the final chapter. Given where you want to be professionally in five years, you may need to get additional training or broaden your experience on the job.

Exercise 25
Action Steps

Broadening Your Experience

- First, identify any professional training you may need to pursue in the near future. Include the names of any people you can approach for support in getting this training, such as your boss (if your company supports professional development) or education and training specialists who can help you get on track with the right courses.

- Do you need to broaden your experience on the job? If so, there may be special assignments or even a job transfer that might help you acquire some of the experience you need to move in the right direction. List potential on-the-job assignments that might broaden your skills. Prepare for a conversation with your boss or other appropriate manager to ask for those assignments. Be sure to use the preparation strategies you learned in this book, with an emphasis on how this experience will benefit the company as well as you individually.

(continued)

Polishing Your Interpersonal Skills

- Identify at least three skills in need of development (for example, learning to cope with conflict, stress management, and customer relations).

- Identify in-house resources who might be able to help you find the appropriate training. There may be other resources as well, such as your community college course catalogue or other sources of training courses in your area.

- After investigating what is available in your area, list courses or training events you wish to take and set a target date for taking them.

- Review the assignments described in the last chapter. Find those that are related to your interpersonal development needs and do them.

- Ask people to recommend readings that might provide you with useful information and skills.

Improving Your Family Life

- Identify at least three things you can do to start enhancing the quality of your life at home. If you are married or in a relationship, this might include something you and your partner (and your children, if any) can do together that will add to the quality of your lives.

- If you are not in a relationship and want to be, list at least three things you can do that will put you in a position to meet a potential partner.

Expanding Your Network of Friends

- Identify at least three people you would like to get to know better. These can be people from work or people you know from other settings.

- Make a commitment to call each of these people and ask him or her to do something socially. This can be anything from going to a ball game to having dinner together.

- See if you can get your co-workers interested in getting together sometime after work hours. This can be as simple as meeting somewhere after work or having a potluck dinner at someone's house. Be sure to invite your boss. Bosses need friends, too.

Service to Your Community

- List at least one way that you can serve your community. Find something in your area that is of interest to you and see how you might get involved. This does not have to represent a major commitment of your time, such as meeting with a child once a week to serve as a Big Brother or Big Sister (although that would be great if you can do it). There are many short-term service opportunities that would allow you to make a difference even in some small way, such as volunteering to assist on the day of your local MS marathon or AIDS walk.

- Make a commitment to yourself that you will do something that contributes to the welfare of others at least once or twice a year. Do more if you can, but do something.

Recreational Activities

- Life is too short to spend all your time working. Identify at least one thing you have always wanted to do (such as jump out of a plane, take a cooking class, or study tai chi) and do it—now!

Other

- Add any other action steps that will help you realize your vision. There may well be other steps you need to take if you are to move in the direction of living your vision. For example, you may need to get some help with diet and exercise or join a health club. Or you may feel a need to deepen your spiritual experience but you've been putting it off. List two or three places to check out and then do it.

Chapter Eleven

Deepening Your Relationships

Up until now, we have focused almost exclusively on building strong professional relationships directed toward one thing—getting the job done. The primary purpose of your relationships on the job is to accomplish work. You are not there to find a family. You are not there to make friends. Your company needs you and your co-workers to work together and get things done. So we have spent a lot of our time together in this book working on the information and skills that will help you build stronger and more appropriate working relationships. But this does not diminish the importance of the personal relationships we develop at work.

You can have it all. You can have wide-open professional relationships. You can argue passionately about differing points of view at work without taking things personally. And you can build warm personal relationships with the people with whom you spend so many of your waking hours five days a week. You're going to be working anyway. Why not fill your days with connection, mutual support, and friendship?

The Opportunity for Human Connection

So much has been written about the isolation that so many people feel in today's society. We used to grow up in small towns and stay there. Friendships and support were readily available. When help was needed, neighbors were there to lend a hand. But we have become a highly mobile society with huge numbers of people living in much larger cities. We move from house to house, from city to city, from job to job. Ironically, much like the Ancient Mariner surrounded by water with nothing to drink, we live surrounded by people, yet many of us report a sense of loneliness and feel cut off from the thousands of people around us.

You may be one of the lucky ones. You may have a large circle of friends to count on when you need them. But many of us live in cities where we don't even know the people in the house next door or in the apartment across the hall. We may greet them and even know their first names, but that is all too often just about as far as it goes.

Where, then, do we look for the interpersonal connections that are so important to us all? We look to our families, certainly, but I am willing to bet that many of the people who read this book are just like me. My closest blood relatives are halfway across the country, and I see them far less often than I would like. Families have become so widely dispersed that the meaning of extended family has almost been lost in the last hundred years.

In my years in Iowa City, I attended a church that recognized the need we all have for this feeling of a group we know as family. They created an "extended family" program. They randomly assigned people to small groups, making sure to include in each a broad range of ages and marital situations. What we did from there was entirely up to each "family." For several years before I left the Midwest, I was blessed with a cluster of people who spent holidays together, went camping, and did all the other things that extended families used to do together. Twenty years later, I still miss the intimacy that developed as we spent time together and got to know each other much like family. Such opportunities to connect with people are all too rare.

Many people make connections with others through church, recreational activities, and community service projects. But the easiest place to meet people and develop friendships is at work. When we work day after day with the same group of people, we are surrounded by opportunities to build friendships that can last for years.

If you are going to spend forty or more hours a week with a group of people, you have an opportunity to develop human connections that should not be missed. Can you imagine how sterile work would be if the only contact we had with people at work was focused solely on the job—if there were no greetings, no conversations about the weekend, no advice on how to deal with your children, no friendships? That is not the kind of organization I would ever want to work for. Life is too short to spend so many of my adult hours in an environment where no one takes the time to get to know and care about each other.

We may work with some of our co-workers for years. This presents us with the opportunity to expand our community of friends and casual acquaintances. We can have it all. We can build professional relationships based on a shared commitment to the work we are working together to accomplish. At the same time, we can establish personal relationships based on mutual respect, caring, and love. Yes, I used the word *love*.

When I think about the jobs I've had, I don't think about the work itself. Rather, I look back, with fondness, on the people I have been privileged to get to know there. Personal connections with people at work can make even the most ordinary day special and meaningful. Someone once asked me if there is anything I dislike about my career. I responded that the only problem with consulting is that just about the time I start to get to know the people I am working with, the project is over. I have to let go of emerging relationships and move on to my next assignment.

A terrible plane crash was in the news in the days I spent writing this chapter. One of the people who died in the crash was from the Seattle area. Her boss was interviewed on the local news. The man was so grief stricken that he could barely talk. He spoke about what a wonderful person she was and how much she would be missed by people at work who loved her. The professional qualities she brought to her work were certainly important, but he wanted to talk about the terrible loss of a dear friend and colleague. He was talking about the human being, not just someone who filled a slot on the organizational chart.

> **In the end,** it's about the lives **we've touched along** the way.

I've mentioned Bob Solum, my friend and professional colleague who died in a diving accident. Many of his clients were present at his memorial service. They wanted to acknowledge Bob, not the great job he had done helping them build their organizations. They spoke of the person they had grown so fond of. They talked about the enthusiasm he brought to his work, his caring, his interest in people around him, and his capacity for listening. They spoke of his humor and his love of juggling. He worked hard and was very good at his job, but the human qualities he brought to those around him made work all the more interesting and entertaining.

Working in organizations presents us with so many opportunities to connect with wonderful people, if only we pay attention and get to know them. Some of them you will work with for years, while others represent brief contacts in the course of getting your work

Exercise 26
Exploring Your Beliefs About the Interpersonal Aspects of Work

- Do a quick inventory of the people you have the most contact with at work. Assess your relationship with each of them on a scale of 1 to 5, with 1 representing no personal closeness at all, and 5 representing intimacy and friendship.

- Make a list of the unwritten rules, beliefs, and attitudes about establishing personal relationships in the workplace. Which of these might limit your willingness to take the risk of developing closer relationships with your co-workers?

- Write a new "rule" that might help you reach out to establish more personal connections at work and thereby enrich your working life.

accomplished. Every person you meet may well be someone worth getting to know. The above exercise will help you open the door to establishing interpersonal connections at work.

Making Contact

When I do team development, I put a lot of emphasis on making a distinction between personal and professional relationships. I then focus on how to build strong and open communication based on professional, rather than personal, needs. I do this for a reason. I think some organization development approaches place too much emphasis on sharing personal feelings and making friendships as the basis of teamwork.

I hope that the work in the first two-thirds of this book has demonstrated the danger of building teams in this way. Conflict about professional issues becomes overly personalized or not talked about at all. Difficult decisions need to be made, such as choosing the right person for a promotion or movement into an interesting job assignment. Unless we are able to separate our professional perspectives from our personal feelings, relationships at work get all tangled up into a web of hurtful and misplaced emotions.

But that is not to say that we need to avoid making personal connections with people at work. On the contrary, the very best working environment is one in which people can work hard and disagree openly about professional issues without taking things personally, all the while caring about each other very much as human beings. Pulling this off successfully takes discipline and the ability to know what's personal and what's not. But it also takes a conscious effort to build and maintain closer, more personal relationships with those around you.

Building friendships takes initiative. If you are a shy person, reaching out is not easy. The following exercises show some simple things to do that will help you break the ice with people at work you would like to get to know better.

Exercise 27
Becoming More Approachable

- Begin by standing in front of a mirror. Take a few deep breaths and look at yourself. What do you see? Does the person in the mirror look friendly and approachable? I, for one, can look pretty serious, even when I am feeling upbeat and happy. I have to remind myself to communicate that to my face.

- While looking in the mirror, try smiling and see the difference. It can change your appearance from someone who might look difficult to approach to someone others might like to get to know. I think you might be surprised by the appearance other people see every day. If your face is sending the wrong message, change the message. For a long time, I kept a mirror hanging by the door of my house. I put it there to remind myself not to look so darned serious all the time.

Exercise 28
Reaching Out to Others

- List at least three people at work you would like to get to know better. Don't be afraid to list your boss.

- Make a commitment to ask at least one of them to share a coffee break or lunch sometime in the next week. If they ask why, tell them you just want to get to know them a little better.

- Tongue-tied and don't know what to talk about? Here is a list of possibilities:

  Ask about their job histories and how they happen to be where they are today.

  Ask about their outside interests and family.

  Ask about where and how they were raised.

  Talk about current events. Anything will do. Just ask questions and listen.

  Talk about yourself in a give-and-take conversation.

  Remember that the purpose of this time together is to get to know a co-worker a bit better personally. This is not a date, so you can relax about this and enjoy yourself.

- Make a list of any new people who have recently joined the company or have just joined your team. Make it a point to welcome them and ask them to share a coffee break with you.

Appropriate Self-Disclosure on the Job

If you want to get closer to people, you have to be willing to reveal enough of yourself so that they will feel close to you. Some people have a great deal of trouble with this at work. They can work with people for years and never say much about themselves. If they also happen to be the kind of people who show little interest in others, they will rightfully be perceived as remote, distant, and hard to get to know. As a manager, this kind of person can be positively scary to work for.

Getting to know people **takes** the **willingness** to be known **by them.**

Self-disclosure involves the willingness to reveal yourself to others. The range of what you can reveal is so broad that some judgment is required about what you reveal to a co-worker, even in the pursuit of friendship and intimacy. I am using the word *intimacy* carefully here. By intimacy, I do not mean anything sexual. Intimacy, as I am using it, is appropriate at work. Intimacy means emotional closeness, caring, warmth, affection, and familiarity. Is it possible for co-workers to share this kind of intimacy and still be able to work effectively? I think it is not only possible, it is desirable. It can help build trust and make it all the easier for people to develop strong and open professional relationships. The more we know each other, the easier it is for us to trust each other's intentions when there are professional disagreements. We are less likely to worry about "hidden agendas" and "politics."

Self-disclosure makes intimacy possible. If we don't know each other, we can't be close to each other. However, some people don't know where to draw the line with self-disclosure in workplace relationships. Too much self-disclosure can be a problem in a number of ways. We all know someone who always seems to be in crisis about something and is more than willing to tell everyone about it—in great detail. Sometimes it can look like people forget that there is work to be done. Personal conversations should be brief and should not intrude on your own or the other person's workday. Longer conversations should be restricted to the lunch period or the coffee shop after work.

It is important to understand that intimacy is a relative term. On one end of the scale is the strictly business stance on relationships. Here, there is little warmth or sharing. We stay focused on the job. The group atmosphere might be distantly polite at best. At its worst, the atmosphere might be chillingly distant and not a very fun place to spend much time. At the other extreme is the kind of openness and warmth you might find between the very closest of friends or lovers. In this kind of relationship, little is withheld. The very nature of the relationship leads each to be willing to be known by the other. Most of our relationships at work will fall between the two extremes of the intimacy scale, and our depth of self-disclosure in these relationships will be somewhat limited.

Some people, in pursuit of closeness at work, don't seem to know where to draw the line. If "strictly business" is a 1 and "closest friendship" is a 10, openness and warmth with friends at work might be something more like a 5 or 6. That means you share a great deal of yourself but probably not everything. The range of things you will share is broad and depends on the person you are dealing with at the time and how much closeness the two of you have developed. With some, self-disclosure might be limited to discussions of weekend activities and current events in the news. With other, more intimate friendships at work, you might talk about struggles you are having with your teenager at home or the happiness you have found in a new relationship.

Your job is not a support group. Endless **public suffering** and emotional crises are **tiresome** and **distracting.**

Caution, however, is appropriate. This is still the workplace. The person you are talking to might one day be your boss, so use discretion in deciding what to share with a co-worker. Some things are better left for relationships outside of work. For example, if you are recovering from an addiction to alcohol or drugs, you might best keep this to yourself. Or you may have been troubled by depression and you are taking medication to control it. While this is a relatively common problem, it is not necessarily something you want other people to know about. Some people might not understand this or be able to put it in its proper context. People like to gossip, so don't make yourself the topic of office conversation by being too willing to disclose what can be damaging personal details.

Those who receive personal information shared at work must treat it with respect. It must never be misused. Unfortunately, people sometimes do. I once did a project in which an employee was being supported in seeking treatment for a problem with alcohol. In a meeting, one executive turned to another and said, "Jim, given your own experience with this problem, maybe you could follow up with him and encourage him to go to AA meetings." This was deeply embarrassing to Jim. He had shared his personal recovery experience with the other person in what he thought was a private, personal conversation. Working in a conservative financial institution, he had never told anyone else about it. Both parties here made an error in judgment. Jim should have kept his history to himself. And the other person should have had the good sense to keep that kind of personal information private.

Making Amends

No matter how much we try not to, most of us mess up from time to time. In the heat of the moment, we may explode in anger. At other times, we may cut people off abruptly and fail to listen as intently as we might intend to. We make promises and fail to keep them. In all kinds of ways, our imperfections and human failings express themselves just as surely at work as they do in the rest of our life.

That we will fail to live up to our own expectations is almost a given. How we handle it when we do is crucial. Relationships are based on trust. When we do things that will undermine that trust, we must clean up the messes we make. That means having the willingness and courage to acknowledge that we were wrong and, in so doing, make amends to the people we have harmed.

To make amends does not mean that you have to grovel and beg for the other person's forgiveness. To make amends means that you are willing to do what is necessary to make something right once again. The best way to do this is to acknowledge what you did and make a promise to do better in the future. Then you have to follow through and keep your promise.

Nothing is more important to maintaining the health of relationships than making amends where they are due. Your willingness to do so will open the door to the repair of trust that might have been damaged by your actions. We are all too willing to just let things blow over. We might even make a silent promise to ourselves to do better next time. Then we live in hope that others will notice the change in our behavior and let bygones be bygones.

Unfortunately, negative impressions die hard. The damage we may have done might live in the memory of the other person long after we think the incident should have been forgotten. Sometimes the only way for a relationship to heal is to acknowledge the damage done, with a promise of more appropriate behavior in the future.

An example from a consulting project provides a lesson in how important this can be. I was working with an executive who had been promoted at a young age. He was surrounded by older, more experienced people whose technical knowledge was much greater than his own. Feeling insecure because of his relative inexperience, he responded by acting as if he knew more than he actually did. His team rapidly grew tired of his unwillingness to listen and his insistence on making decisions based on little information and even less knowledge. By the time I got involved with the team, he had just about used up his credibility and was about to lose his job.

We explored the importance of making amends. He made a list of all the relationships in need of repair. He made a series of appointments to talk to each person on the list privately. But it is important to understand what he did in these meetings. He did not rend his garments and beg for forgiveness. Instead, he said something like this:

I want you to know that I know that I haven't lived up to my own standards of listening and collaborative teamwork in recent months. You have more experience in your specialty than I will ever have, and I haven't been giving you the chance to give me the advice I so desperately need. I promise to turn this around, as of now.

Then he let each person know that the team would start having regular staff meetings, designed as an opportunity for his team to offer their input on decisions needing to be made. This series of individual and team meetings created a turning point that salvaged the young man's position. It did so only because he had the courage to admit that he was wrong, and then he followed through with the promises he made. Making amends without follow-through is empty. You don't get many second chances with people before they quit listening and trust is irrevocably broken.

Note that the young executive did not ask for forgiveness. At least two of his managers were quite upset and might not have given their forgiveness easily. They would have been uncomfortable with even being asked for it. The only appropriate thing for the executive to do was

Exercise 29
Cleaning Up Your Messes

• Make a list of people you may have harmed through action or inaction.

• For each person, describe what you did and what you are going to do to make sure this doesn't repeat itself in the future.

• Set an appointment to meet with each person on your list and then do what you promised to do.

acknowledge what he had done and make good on his promises. Sometimes forgiveness and the rebuilding of trust must be earned—and this takes time, not just a handshake.

If you are anything like the rest of us, you probably have a relationship or two that has been strained by something you did or failed to do. Don't put off making any amends that might be due. The above exercise can help you begin repairing the damage you may have done.

The Gift of Acknowledgment

Perhaps the most effective way to build relationships can be summed up in two words: "Thank you." I am astonished how often people tell me how much they hunger to be acknowledged for the work they do. In fact, study after study of job satisfaction shows that the expression of appreciation is one of the things people want most from their manager.

This is just as true of personal relationships. If you want to develop more closeness with people on your team, you must express your appreciation of them and the things they do. How else are they to know that they make a difference in your life and that you appreciate them?

You can express appreciation for what people do both personally and professionally. Your boss, for example, may do a great job of keeping you informed. She may take great care to give away decision-making authority whenever possible and to be open to input on decisions where she has retained the decision-making authority. You may have a co-worker who volunteered to stay late and help out one night when you had gotten behind in your work. Or another co-worker may have done an extraordinary job in one of the team's projects. People on the job are always doing things that present you with an opportunity to express appreciation.

There are also people in your working life who make an almost immeasurable difference in the quality of your life from day to day. I am talking about the personal qualities they bring to their work. Most of us have those favorite people whose presence would be so missed if they weren't there. When I think back on my life at work, I can remember so many people whose energy, enthusiasm, and personality made work much more enjoyable. There was Mike, a fellow psychologist at the mental health facility where I worked. Mike was one of those rare people whose humor and optimism always made even the darker days brighter. He had a large "port wine stain" birthmark on one hand. Sometimes, working with a group of patients he would say, "Oh, no! Not again." He would stare at his hand and then grab his own throat with it and act like he was struggling to get it loose with his other hand. It never failed to get a laugh because that was Mike. How could I not have a better day being around someone who brought a sense of joy and play into even very serious work?

People need to hear how much you appreciate the gift they are in your life.

Then there was my friend Bob, who I have mentioned a couple of times in this writing. I have never known anyone with such a capacity for listening. He was intensely interested in so many things. It was always enjoyable to spend time with him. Conversations ranged from new discoveries in physics to education reform. And often as not, he would be practicing his patented behind-the-back juggling moves and laughing about the latest weird story he'd read in the paper. How could I not enjoy work when spending time with someone who brought so much attention to everything he did?

I could go on and on about people I met at work and grew to love and appreciate over time. And so, I'll bet, could you. People who enhance the quality of your life deserve to hear from you. But if you are going to acknowledge someone, do it effectively. A vague statement that you really like someone is nice to hear, but you can give someone much more powerful acknowledgment if you express your appreciation more specifically. Praise, to avoid sounding vague or even phony, needs to include two components:

- First, describe some specific thing the other person did that you appreciate.
- Second, talk about why you appreciate it.

Here are some examples:

Ted, I really appreciate the call you made to me when you heard that my wife was in the hospital. I was feeling alone and down at the time and your call really boosted my spirits. Thanks so much for reaching out to me.

Marie, I've always wanted to tell you how much I enjoy working with you. You are always smiling and upbeat. I think you add an element of enthusiasm that really sparks our team.

Don't miss the opportunity to let those around you know how much you appreciate them. When I lead retreats, I use an exercise in acknowledgment that has never failed to work. After talking about some of the people I worked with in the past who contributed so much to my life, I comment on how we can often go years without telling those around us how much we love and appreciate them. Then I describe what I am about to ask the retreat participants to do:

In a moment, I am going to ask you all to stand and come to the center of the room at the same time. Then I want you to get to as many people as you can in the short time allowed and express your appreciation of them. This can involve something they have done professionally that was noteworthy. Or it can be more personal, such as something someone did

Exercise 30
Expressing Appreciation

- Make a list of at least ten people you have regular contact with at work.

- For each person, list something he or she has done recently that you appreciate, either personally or professionally.

- Also describe why you appreciate this particular thing. What is the impact this person is having on your life at work?

- Make a point of expressing your appreciation the next time you see him or her. You might start with something like, "Mary, there is something I have been wanting to share with you." Then tell the person what you have to say.

that you especially liked or perhaps something about their way of being that you have always liked but have never told them about. Make your expression of appreciation quick. While you are speaking, someone will be waiting for you to finish, and there will be others you will want to get to.

As I am giving the instructions, there are always a few people who look as if they would like to slowly sink into the floor or find some other way to escape from the room. Giving and receiving the gift of acknowledgment sounds scary and too intimidating to some people. But once the exercise gets started, energy fills the room. People are shaking hands, hugging, and, sometimes, crying. How strange and how sad it is that the simple gift of appreciation is so rarely given that people are moved to tears when finally it is given freely and with love.

There are many people whose mere presence makes your day better. And so many others do things for you professionally and personally that make your life at work so much more satisfying. Isn't it about time you let them know how much they mean to you?

Love and Work

Yes, you can have it all. You can have wide open professional relationships. You can argue passionately about differing points of view at work without taking things personally. And you can build warm personal relationships with the people you spend so many of your waking hours with five days a week. You're going to be working anyway. Why not fill your days with love, intimacy, mutual support, and friendship? The choice is yours.

Index

Co-workers (continued)
guidelines for working with, 83–84; importance of conversations, 7–8; intimacy sharing by, 166; making amends to, 168–170; personal contact with, 164–165; personal logic of, 54–56; problems interacting with, 1; remembrances of, 11–12; social involvement with, 160; unawareness of impact on others, 52–53. See also Conflict; Personal history; Personal relationships; "Problem people"; Professional relationships; Work relationships

Customer service, company assumptions regarding employee's abilities, 29

Decision making: communication to team members regarding decision, 96–97; consulting role in, 94–96, 98–99, 102; hierarchical nature of, 91; risk and, 92–93; roles in, 90

Defense reaction, for conflict, 32

Development of individual. See Personal development

Disagreement: effect on teamwork, 73; personal history effects on, 109; regarding authority, 92; regarding conflict with individual, guidelines for addressing,144–145;

Diversity, 57–58

Emotions: raising the issue and, 143; response to conflict; 140–142. See also Anger; Fear

Errors, worker versus system as cause of, 86–87

Expectations: defining of, 75–76; failure of, amends for, 168; in personal relationships, 13

Explosive conflict, 32–33

Failure of expectations: amends for, 168; in personal relationships, 13

Family-based businesses: case studies of relationships in, 22–24; challenges associated with, 21; dynamics of, 20; supervision of family members, 20

Fear: effect of personal history on, 109; of expressing appreciation, 173; as response to conflict, 109–111

Feedback, conversation for eliciting: avoidance of defensive reaction, 156–157; peer involvement, 154; personal behavior during, 155–157; preparations, 154–157; questions to ask, 154–155, 158; sample structure, 157, 159; scheduling of, 155

Feelings. See Emotions; Personal feelings

Firings, common reasons for, 3

Forgiveness, 169–170

Friendships: building of, 162, 165; expanding your network of, 160

Frustrations: from decision maker's inability to make decision, 92; personalizing of, 5; sources of, 5

Goals: identification of, 74–75; team agreement regarding, 70–75

Good intentions, nature of, 44–47; self-sabotage of, factors that contribute to, 51–58; trust and, 48, 144

Gossip, 167

Growth of organization, relationship challenges associated with: approaches to, 81–82; case study, 79–81; description of, 78; ways to deal with, 81–82

Helplessness: "payoffs" of, 48–49; prevalence of, 48–49. See also Victim

History, of individual. See Personal history

Impact of conflict: methods of conveying, 119–124; statements, 123–124, 136–137

Inefficiency, worker versus system as cause of, 86–87

Intentions. See Good intentions

Interpersonal procedures, 76–77

Interpersonal skills: evaluation of, 160; importance of, 3; lack of training in, 29; for leadership position, 3; questions to elicit feedback regarding, 158; success and, 29; for team participation, 29

Bob Wall

Bob Wall has been a full-time independent consultant and trainer since 1980. He is based in the Seattle area, but his work has taken him across the country into a broad variety of settings. His clients range from large corporations to small and midsized organizations in the public and private sectors. His work brings him into contact with members at every level of his clients' organizations, from company presidents and leadership teams to entry-level staff.

Bob specializes in organizational assessment, strategic planning, and leadership and team development. He is also available for specialized presentations, such as breakout sessions or keynotes at association meetings. To learn more about how he might be of service to you, give him a call. He will assess your needs carefully and help you decide whether he is a good fit for your particular situation and then work closely with you to tailor the project or presentation to your group. Don't hesitate to call; Bob loves talking with people on the phone about work and the challenges of working relationships.

If you would like a full-sized copy of the two raising issues worksheets presented in this book, send a self-addressed, stamped envelope to the address listed below. Please include a donation of $5 or more made out to the National Multiple Sclerosis Society (not mandatory, but much appreciated).

You have read the book. Now you can lead the workshop. If you are a trainer, look for Bob's book *The Handbook for Interpersonal Skills Training,* scheduled for release by McGraw-Hill in 2000. This book contains everything you need for training events ranging in length from two hours to two days, focusing on the information and skills presented in *Working Relationships* (and a book on leadership and performance management, tentatively scheduled for release in late 2000). The handbook will provide you with workshop designs, lecture notes, overheads, and participant handouts. You will be able to deliver a powerful training and offer participants their own copy of *Working Relationships* to reinforce their learning experience. Contact Davies-Black Publishing for information on discounts for bulk orders.

Bob Wall can be reached at:
Bob Wall & Associates
8845 North Town Drive
Bainbridge Island, WA 98110
(206) 780-2919
(206) 780-0528 (fax)
bobwall@nwlink.com (e-mail)